Rapid
Change

For Busy Heart-Centered
Women Who Want to Be
the Best Version of
Themselves

Compiled by
LORETTA MOHL

CM Publisher
c/o Marketing for Coach, Ltd
Second Floor
6th London Street
W2 1HR London (UK)

www.cm-publisher.com
info@cm-publisher.com

ISBN: 978-0-9928173-7-4

Published in UK, Europe, US and Canada

Book Cover: Csernik Előd

Inside Layout: Csernik Előd

Table of Contents

Foreword

If only we knew, in the midst of pain or witnessing trauma, that these experiences would be essential to our soul's evolution. Who in their right mind would choose to create such chaos and endure such darkness? We go through life waiting, wishing, and hoping for change. Expecting others to love us, nurture us, understand us, or meet some need we believe we lack.

Most of our lives we search to find ourselves. Try endlessly to find our purpose or who we are. We become scattered in our thinking, spinning in life looking for the best relationship, the best body, the best friend, the best education. The whole time we are looking outside of ourselves. Some part of us believes other people's responses and reactions define who we are.

You will be happy to learn that's all BS! Never again do you need to let anyone define who you are! You, my friend, are an entity of your own creation. Yes, you have created this life of yours based on your experiences. Following your way to your heart center requires little time but a big commitment.

Commitment to you! You are the love you are looking for. You are the relationship you desire. You are everything you hope for and aspire to be. It is you and only you who has to define who you are.

In 2009, Loretta Mohl created a system known as FIT which teaches people how to identify, root out and eliminate limiting beliefs. Loretta,

1

founder of Focused Intention Technique, has developed an easy 11-step process to spiral into the heart center and awaken the absolute truth. Once you become aware of your innermost truth, you awaken every cell in your body to the vibration of the truth, thus healing the cells in your body. No longer does the pain from our body affect us mentally, emotionally, physically and spiritually. We come to realize we are not the stories we have held in our belief system. Loretta has been known to some as the belief slayer and a catalyst for growth.

"Rapid Change" is a book for busy heart-centered women who want to be the best version of themselves. It is a compilation of writings by 30 passionate and brilliant women who have worked to transform themselves into all they can be. Healing holistically requires you to know yourself mentally, emotionally, physically and spiritually. Each chapter is an opportunity to embrace YOU and transform all four power areas of your life.

Find the passion in life, seek out your purpose and never allow your opportunities to be limited. Loretta allowed herself to remove fear by doing difficult personal inner work, and now teaches heart-centered women around the world how to break free from the shackles of their limiting beliefs. Loretta has shared, "All women are beautiful, and we will change the world when we feel comfort in our skin, our power, and our possibilities. I believe living life in alignment with our purpose is the biggest gift we can give ourselves and the world. I believe in giving great service to others; I believe we are perfect, whole and complete just the way we are. Own that and it will change your life. I believe life becomes so much richer when we connect to or create our own movement and work on it fiercely to change the world."

We love you Loretta,

Jane Burning
Six Nations of the Grand River
Ohsweken, Ontario

Gratitude

I created this anthology for many reasons, but the main two were first, to let women know they have choices. They can make rapid changes in their life and become their best self. The second reason was to tap into the power of collaborating with other women who share my passion.

To the amazing co-authors who shared in this experience, thank you. And thank you to all the many people who have assisted in bringing this book into being. Your hearts, gifts, and dedication made this book possible, and I'm so grateful to have had this opportunity to share our passions and common mission. I love you all.

I am blessed to be surrounded by so many extraordinary people in my life. Without them it would not be possible for me to do what I do and to advance my mission of helping people live their highest lives. For all who have helped in the shaping of my ideas, encouraged me to dream big, and aided in spreading my message, I am deeply grateful.

And thank you to the amazing men in my life: my spouse, Francis, for his endless love and support, and my son, Corey, for his joy and encouragement.

A final thanks to my incredible publishing team, especially Christine Marmoy. Thank you for being such an inspiration and joy throughout the process. Christine is a true role model for every business woman around the world, and she's taught me how to maximize the power of collaboration and to stand in your truth and shine your light.

Rapid Results Whole Self Wheel

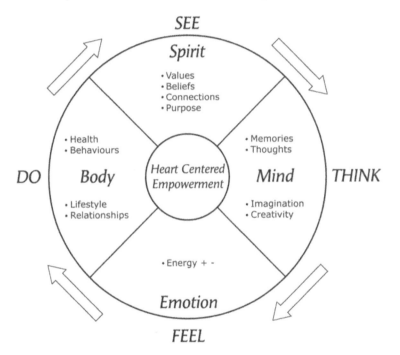

SEE

Spirit

· Values
· Beliefs
· Connections
· Purpose

· Health
· Behaviours

· Memories
· Thoughts

DO

Body

Heart Centered Empowerment

Mind

THINK

· Lifestyle
· Relationships

· Imagination
· Creativity

· Energy + -

Emotion

FEEL

Introduction to the Whole Self: Our Entirety: Mentally, Emotionally, Physically, Spiritually

The book you are about to read is not your everyday book. Its pages are designed to be written upon and creased. There is nothing clean and tidy about embarking on a personal transformation. To get the most out of your journey prepare to make it your own.

Through these lessons the authors present you tools, tips, and strategies to achieve greater well-being, happiness and fulfillment, to live the best version of you. For a majority of my career I have dedicated myself to helping others transform their lives. It's my passion. It gives me life and energy.

It has been my mission to assist personal transformation towards discovering your purpose and living the life you love. This book is my latest step in my journey. I have had many moments that have spurred me towards transformation. From facing personal struggles in my childhood, to having to take care of my addicted grandfather dying of cancer, to the sudden death of my husband.

Working on my own personal transformation hasn't always been easy, and that is why my focus for you is to make rapid change easy and possible. That's why I've compiled this book.

When most women look in the mirror, we tend to narrow in on our trouble spots, scrutinizing what could be better, rather than loving the beauty of our whole self – body, mind, heart, and soul. Then this mindset consumes us and affects us when we look inward—we find and agonize over all the things we don't like about ourselves, rather than embracing our whole self. But when a woman's body, mind, heart, and soul are all in sync and focused on the positives, anything is possible.

So how are we to do it? How do we reach this best version of ourselves? Well, first we must meet our so-called faults and befriend them with love. To do this, it is crucial to engage with the following lessons in this book. These lessons were created by 30 women experts who know how to make change easy and uncomplicated, and know what systems work best to develop the whole self so that we can manifest all that we desire, while being the best version of ourselves we can. These women know to how to make change easy and uncomplicated, because each author has her own powerful story about experiencing drastic change in order to find meaning and fully realign her life.

The first step to being the best we can be is to understand the Whole Self Model. The model can essentially be grouped into four major facets, or potentials: we see (spiritual), we think (mental), we feel (emotional), and we do (physical). These four potentials work together to make us who we are. As we go through life, all of these facets will interact, so if we are developing each one in a balanced way – paying attention to all four potentials – then we have a greater opportunity to be at our best. This is the opportunity the lessons in this book will provide, so get ready because the best version of you awaits!

Loretta Mohl

Self-Limiting Belief Buster Loretta Mohl is, the creator of the Focused Intention Technique (FIT) that has guided hundreds of women since 1998 to live lives they love through the power of listening, reflecting, and gaining clarity around the intentions that matter most for each. She is the author of "Bust Your Stress: Heal Your Past and Get a Move on Life," "Bust Your Stress: Heal Your Past to Get Your Happiness On," and "Unlimited You."

Playa del Carmen, Mexico

www.lorettamohl.com

(1) 780-910-5052 or **(52) 984-130-2681**

lorettam11

lorettamohl@gmail.com

facebook.com/ResetMindsetExpert

facebook.com/ResetMindsetExpert

linkedin.com/in/lorettamohl

LESSON 1

HOW TO MASTER THE FOUR LEVELS OF THE HOLISTIC MODEL: FROM RESISTANCE TO RAPID CHANGE

By Loretta Mohl

"We do not become more organized by purchasing a filing cabinet. We do not become more healthy by joining a gym. We don't even become more at ease in our lives by speaking with a therapist. In order to enact change, we must choose to act, and it's that action that drives the change, making the difference."

~ James Clear

What prevents us from living the life we want, from becoming who we want to be, from doing what we desire, and from having what we wish? The answer is this – our limiting beliefs. These beliefs directly affect our thoughts, our emotions, and what we do. And though we know that change on a whole-self level can take time, there are components to the whole-self model that can be changed rapidly.

I'm living the life I love and after eliminating my blocks, I manifested an abundance of amazing and supportive friends. I now live in a place I had always dreamed of – near the beach in Playa del Carmen, Mexico, and I've met the most incredible man who is a true partner to me in every way. The work I do is my passion and it is also an enjoyment for me to do. However, this wasn't always the case.

I've had to work through and eliminate a lot of limiting beliefs – beliefs that I adopted as a child like: "I'm not good enough," or "I'm unworthy of love," or "My parents would love me more I had been a boy." You see, at the time my mother got pregnant with me, my parents had two children—both girls—and they were hoping their third (me) would be a boy. Then I was born, and ever since I've had to work through self-worth issues and the fact that I was always trying to prove myself to my father. The beliefs I established about myself not being enough stem from this, and they were the exact beliefs I had to eliminate as I got older.

Working through this on a personal level allowed me to identify a process that would eliminate these negative core beliefs for others, as well. After spending years researching and working with clients, I designed a powerful and effective rapid change therapy – Focused Intention Technique (FIT) – to laser in on the root cause of problematic issues that reside deep within a person's subconscious. Bringing these issues to the forefront of the conscious mind allows them to be resolved and eliminated forever. This then allows a person's beliefs, values, connectedness, and purpose to shift and develop into positive, self-actualization. In other words, they go from living life to loving life and awakening their best self.

So how do you reach this best self? Well, first you must meet your so-called faults and befriend them with love. If you want to be happy, your goal must be to remove your self-created blocks that prevent you from accessing your happiness. Happiness is a common goal for most people, and it's often absent from so many people's lives because at one point, they developed a belief that now prevents their access to inherent happiness. It may sound hard to believe that one belief can do so much, but it can – it can cloud your perceptions on life, can slow your energies, and can attract further negative experiences. And it can and should be changed.

Access to your happiest energies links directly to the intelligent force of intention. So when you work more and more with focused intention and it becomes clear that you are encountering and collaborating, your energies become vibrant, and so does your health on the spiritual, mental, emotional, and physical levels – alignment on all levels!

THE POWER OF ALIGNMENT

People, habits, patterns, emotions, miscommunications, they all have a role to play in our journey to be the best version of ourselves. It's all connected, everything, everyone. Our experiences don't happen by accident; every experience connects us to a powerful lesson that will bring us closer to what we desire, closer to our best self.

All of the healing and releasing I've done over the years has aligned me so I can show up – really show up – in my life. And that's exactly what I want for you! Alignment is about letting go of what no longer serves you so you can express the most authentic version of yourself. I've experienced numerous emotions that at times felt upsetting and off-putting, but without them, I'd never have learned to speak my truth, to own my value, and to stand up for what I believe.

But I was ready to start changing things in my life so I could be my best self. Are you? I was deliberate, I was fiercely devoted to moving through my resistance so that I could get to the point where I felt comfortable being visible in the world and free of those once limiting beliefs.

Our alignment can essentially be grouped into four major facets of the Holistic Model: we see (spiritual), we think (mental), we feel (emotional), and we do (physical). These four facets work together to make us who we are. Just as a human body has different parts – heart, brain, legs, fingers, hands, etc. – which individually need to be healthy for the physical body to do its best work, it is the same with the spiritual, mental, emotional, and physical parts of ourselves. They each need to be nurtured, developed, and exercised in order for our self to function at its best.

As we go through life, what we think will interact with what we feel, and what we feel will interact with what we do, all parts connected and working together. So when we develop each in a balanced way, we have a greater opportunity to be at our best. When, however, we have even one undeveloped part – say emotional for instance – then our whole self would parallel a damaged wheel, a wheel that when moved would move forward in a bumpy way, slowing its progress. As the wheel turned, each aspect would be affected by the damaged part. So if you apply this concept to the whole self, you can see how if one part is out of alignment, it can affect all the other parts of the self.

FIVE TIPS TO ALIGN YOUR WHOLE SELF

1. Examine your core beliefs and values, your relationships, and your purpose in life. Think about these things, reflect on them, and write down what limiting beliefs you have and where you think those beliefs originated. Next, think about your relationships with your family, neighbors, and community. What are those relationships like? Have they ever shifted or changed over the years? If so, what caused the changes? And lastly, consider your purpose. Who are you? Where do you belong? Why do you exist?

2. Find appropriate and meaningful ways to allow your emotions to surface. Accept your emotions (if there are any you're hiding from, you need to connect to them), make a list of them and explain why you feel you need to hide them. Also, indicate what it was that triggered this emotion. Then rewrite each emotion with "I felt" in front of it. When you use the "I" statement, you communicate the fact that you are choosing your emotional response, while also building your awareness that you are empowered to choose your response.

3. Answer the following: How well do you take care of yourself? Do you eat the foods and nutrients your body needs? Do you exercise regularly? Do you make sure to get enough sleep? If you answered no to any of these, why? And are there any beliefs causing you to believe that your real self does not deserve to exist? If so, what experiences created these beliefs?

4. Create healthy, daily habits. At the start of each day, create a clear and powerful intention by focusing on your goals for the day. Post a reminder to your desk or set a reminder on your phone – either way, remember that energy follows thought and that this is a crucial step in becoming the best you.

5. Calm your central nervous system (CNS), deactivate your fight or flight system, and reconnect to your body, soul, and heart with a 5 second exercise—the FIT Zone. To get in the

FIT Zone, place your right hand on your heart and activate thoughts of safety and security to calm the CNS. Practice this heart-centered connection throughout the day so you effectively restructure the brain, the body, and the CNS to respond differently. You can also do the exercise whenever you feel overwhelmed, stressed, frustrated, unsafe, unsure, lost, lonely, or tired.

Each and every one of you deserves to be happy and confident in her life and body. These tips are strategies that will help you get there. So get ready for a journey and an experience unlike any before. With intention, you can live a life beyond any you've ever experienced before.

Rapid Results Whole Self Wheel

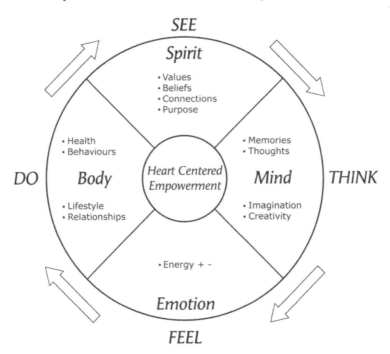

SEE

Spirit
- Values
- Beliefs
- Connections
- Purpose

DO

Body
- Health
- Behaviours

Heart Centered Empowerment

Mind

THINK
- Memories
- Thoughts

- Lifestyle
- Relationships

- Imagination
- Creativity

- Energy + -

Emotion

FEEL

Rapid Change

Introduction:
Be the Best Version of You Spiritually

Let's start by first defining spirituality. Spirituality is a human potential that develops through nurturing, learning, and practice. Our spirituality, therefore, is our vision of relationships, of the world, and of ourselves because what we experience and see – beliefs, values, connectedness, purpose – create our reality.

Many of us women believe, "I'm not good enough," or "I'm too stupid," or "I don't belong here." And too many times we allow thoughts like these to form our belief system. Then we live with these beliefs instead of addressing and eliminating them.

We must know that we don't have to live with negative beliefs like these. All of us can eliminate them and develop our beliefs, values, connectedness, and purpose into positive self-actualization. And in doing so, we enhance our spirituality, getting one step closer to being the best version of ourselves.

The first step to eliminating any limiting beliefs begins now. Read through the lessons in this section. Reflect on them, work through them, make notes, and remember that all change takes time.

Jane Burning

Jane Burning, Haudenosaunee of the Seneca Nation, Bear Clan, is from Six Nations, Ontario. She is a certified Social Service Worker with certification in an array of energy modalities including EMDR Therapist, Reiki Master/Practitioner, Reality Therapy, Psycho Dramatic Body Worker and Focused Intention Technique Practitioner and Trainer, with over 20 years of experience in counseling and facilitation. Currently Jane fulfills contracts with agencies, non-profit organizations and is seen as an elder/mentor for a variety of organizations.

For more detailed information regarding Jane's services please go to her website **www.janeburning.com**

Ohsweken, Ontario, Canada

1(519) 445 1904 or 1(519)732 8806

jane.burning1

info@janeburning.com

facebook.com/JaneBurningHolisticConsultingServices

ca.linkedin.com/pub/jane-burning/18/75a/377

AWAKENING THE SACRED BUNDLE

By Jane Burning

Never before did I think how beautiful grief can be in the midst of it all until I discovered the sacred bundle. At five years old I witnessed my six year old brother die before my eyes. I was terrified, but not certain why. Watching his lifeless body wither to the end, I knew, even at five, I was about to enter a darkness so incredibly painful.

Was this the day he died? Might want to add some clarification if not. Like, "Only a few months before ..." It was a warm fall day; I laid with my brother, Danny, on the ground. We looked up at the sky and peacefully watched the clouds roll by, picking out images of objects, laughing, talking and loving. I never knew until years later, this moment was a time in which I received the greatest teaching in my life. The love I shared with my brother was so incredibly pure. Danny was such an old soul, who had so much inherent wisdom. As we laid there on the ground our heads touching one another, I was later shown how he downloaded his gift of wisdom to me. Through the vibration of his soul, he shared the truth with me.

This truth I speak of has been a process by which I awakened the sacred bundle within my heart center. Despite the darkness and grief that followed my brother's death, I later came to realize that my parents trusted me to raise myself, they knew their role in my life was to birth me and they did just that. Somewhere deep within their subconscious they also knew the power within me by letting me discover the truth.

Most of my childhood was painful due to absent parents, abuse and emotional neglect. As a child, it appeared to me that everyone around me was frozen, except for creation. It was creation who saved me from the psychological effects of this trauma. When I needed to be held, I found myself lying on the ground, embraced by my mother the earth. When I needed to be calmed I asked the wind to wrap around me and comfort me with its gentleness. When I needed someone to talk to I spoke to the animals and they spoke back. I thought this was normal. I thought everyone could do this. These abilities to connect to something greater than the pain, I now realize is a gift from the bundle. This connection is a part of the truth. Unfortunately, the blanket of grief was too heavy and it eventually clouded my vision. The next several years led me to a world of addiction and self-destructive behaviors. I prayed daily for death to enter my body. I did not feel worthy of life.

One of my mentors, born Shaman of the Wet'suwet'en Nation, Frank Austin (Many Horses), asked, "When did you know your life was going to be different?" I responded immediately, by saying, I knew my life would be different when I started to pray to live rather than to die. When my prayers changed, I knew it was divine intervention.

This happened the day I was curled up in the back seat of my car, unable to move due to tremendous fear in my body. It felt like I had no skin, like everyone around me could see all the abuse I suffered in childhood. There was nowhere safe to turn to but inside my own being. Life for me began this day! This spiritual awakening caused me to go inside. I had nowhere else to go but inside, to my sacred bundle. This is what saved me, and helped me find sobriety and recovery. They are not one and the same. Recovery involves being conscious and accountable for all my actions and reactions. I began to meditate and pray on a daily basis, becoming more and more in alignment to the bundle within my heart center.

The awakening of the sacred bundle has allowed me to know the truth within every cell in my body. My greatest discovery is that birth is to death as death is to birth. There is no difference, both are a celebration. When we can see beyond the pain in this earthly realm, and embrace the truth, the pain has no power over us. Yes, it is sad when we lose a dear one, however it is only a part of our existence. The pain is not us in totality. It is not who we are. When we allow ourselves to connect with our heart center we can begin to awaken the truth and see a bigger picture.

Each of us has been gifted life; we in fact have co-created our life. We converse with Creator and co-create our sacred contract. This contract has never been a dictation of our life but a co-creation. We learned at this time what the lessons would be for us here in this earthly realm. When we come into physical form, we are pure. We have within our heart center the sacred bundle full of all the gifts we need to get through the lessons in life. We have Creator's three breaths of life and we know what our lessons are. There is no fear, doubt or resistance from our soul, as our soul knows the truth. It is our calling to the truth that awakens the sacredness within our soul. Creator, God, Source Energy, whichever you chose to call the divine life force did not send us here to endure only pain, but to awaken the truth in our heart center. Life is meant to discover the lessons and awaken the gifts in our bundle.

There truly is no greater vibration than that within our heart center. Emotions in this earthly realm are merely energy. We can begin by seeing energy as a vibration which teaches us how to be in alignment with our soul. All emotions carry a vibration. When we embrace our painful truths from our stories, we are embracing lower vibration's energy. We then become the pain body rather than the purity. Making a conscious effort to embrace the spiritual truth in our stories allows us to raise our vibration and become the sacredness within our bundle.

One of the lessons I have learned is even when I'm in a low vibration energy, I have free will. I can choose to be a victim to my story and be sickened with disease – mentally, emotionally, physically and spiritually – or I can choose to be my own sacredness. In the truth my brother gave me, I have discovered how beautiful death is. There is a thin veil between the physical and spiritual realm, our loved ones are here among us to continue to guide us and hold a loving space for us in a spiritual existence. The only difference is they are not in this physical realm as we have known them to be.

My purpose is to share the beauty in the heart center when we awaken the sacred bundle. By allowing yourself an opportunity to see beyond this physically painful body you will awaken the bundle in its purest form. It really is about choice. Listed below are the steps you can take to Awakening the Sacred Bundle:

1. Be ready for the awakening; listen to the calling of your soul. It will speak to you through addiction, loneliness, grief and despair. Don't miss out on opportunities that present themselves as darkness.

2. Choose to be present in your life; be consciously connected to your Source, Creator, God. Gratitude for all of life's lessons, as painful as they may be, is important, because this will allow you to surrender control.

3. Begin to make a conscious effort to align your mind, body, soul, and spirit through meditation, thus allowing you to receive insight in its purest form.

4. See yourself as a sacred being striving to raise your vibration. Know without a doubt that the truth is alive and well within your heart center. By doing so, you become the truth.

5. Remember the awakening begins with you. It has always been about you. Love is life, and the beauty you see around you is a reflection of you. Stop looking outside of yourself.

Rapid change happens when we live consciously connected to our sacred bundle. It is a calling for us to live; to awaken our truth as if we are seeing the world through the eyes of our soul.

Kimberly Coots

Kimberly Coots is a purpose-driven business and life coach. Her passion is to help women experience fulfillment and make a positive impact in the world through living their true potential.

She is the author of the best-selling book "Divine Worth" and she enjoys speaking on the subjects of self worth, purpose and potential.

Kimberly is the CEO of Promote Your Purpose, and she teaches heart-centered entrepreneurs how to start their own business and promote their purpose online to serve more people and make money doing what they love.

For more information, connect with Kimberly at:

www.PromoteYourPurpose.com

facebook.com/PromoteYourPurpose

twitter.com/KimberlyCoots

youtube.com/PromoteYourPurpose

25

LESSON 3

FIVE KEY INSIGHTS TO LIVING YOUR LIFE PURPOSE

By Kimberly Coots

Is there a part of you that searches for the answer to the innate question of "Why am I here?" Do you find yourself desiring greater meaning and fulfillment in your life? Do you sometimes experience the meaning and fulfillment you seek, but find it to be fleeting?

Many people search for meaning and fulfillment through external sources such as their roles, material gain and approval from others. In this chapter, I'm going to share with you how you can experience meaning and fulfillment through your core (life) purpose which emanates from inside of you, and how to discover what your core purpose is.

Women are commonly conditioned to believe that their role is to nurture others. As mothers, wives, community caregivers and more, it is easy for women to define themselves through their roles. There is nothing wrong with serving these roles, however, it is imperative to do so from a sense of joy and purpose while maintaining your own sense of self.

WHAT IS "PURPOSE"?

The dictionary defines purpose as "the reason for which something exists." Throughout humanity's existence, we've searched for the answer to why we are here and what we're meant to do.

While the answers to those questions are deeply personal to each individual, I'd like to share with you my perspective on it, and invite you to explore yours. I'm going to share with you five key insights to living your purpose, as well as common causes and misconceptions that block you from truly living your purpose.

YOUR DIVINE PURPOSE

In Chapter Four of my best-selling book, "Divine Worth," I talk about what I believe you are…which is a divine spark of Creator (God, Goddess, Universe, All That Is, Source – whichever name you prefer to give to the source of our existence…I will use them interchangeably). Being that you are a divine spark or essence of All That Is, your divine purpose is to experience and create.

The nature or essence of God/Goddess is to experience and create, and that is your innate nature as well. So from the grand, divine perspective, you exist for the purpose of experiencing and creating your divine nature, which is limitless! That also means that your true potential is limitless!

Key Insight #1: Your divine purpose is to experience and create.

While I believe we all share this grand, divine purpose, I also believe we have our individual **core purpose**.

WHAT IS "CORE PURPOSE"?

Your core purpose is what lights you up, brings meaning and fulfillment to your life, and makes you feel alive.

There are two common misconceptions that people make about their core purpose, which can block them from connecting to and fulfilling it.

See if you can relate to these misconceptions and feelings at some point in your life:

- **The belief that your purpose is a job, career or role**
- **The belief that you need to achieve something(s) to be successful**

Let's look at why these beliefs actually block you from connecting with your core purpose:

Key Insight #2: Your core purpose is not a job, career or role.

These functions are only a means to experience or carry out your purpose. I can't tell you how long I spent trying to figure out what I was so supposed to "be" to find meaning and fulfillment in my life.

I could fill almost an entire page with a list of certifications I have (in many areas) over my lifetime of trying to figure out what I am supposed to "be." I have certifications and businesses for: holistic healing, massage therapy, ordained minister, shamanism, best-selling author, fitness trainer, business coaching, marketing, corporate professional and more.

It wasn't until I realized what my core purpose is, and that each of these "roles" allows me to carry out my purpose, that I stopped searching outside of myself, discovered true fulfillment, and really helped people in big ways.

The reason I'm sharing this with you is that I want to make a key point: although my businesses may appear to be very different from each other, they all embody my core purpose, which is connecting and inspiring.

Key Insight #3: Your core purpose is not a role (noun)...it is an innate action (verb).

There are many, many ways you can fulfill your purpose...your job, business or roles are the vehicles in which you can live out your core purpose.

When I realized this, it shifted my entire perspective about my purpose! Rather than trying to find my purpose outside of me through a job, role or career, I realized it was inside of me all along!

To shift out of the second misconception, it's important to realize that **fulfillment is not about getting and having (achieving).** Most of us are conditioned to believe that we have to achieve certain things, such as a lucrative career, family, white picket fence and a large bank account, and that achieving these things means that you are "successful."

The problem with this "success model" is that it is all about self-gain…getting and having, which focuses on appeasing the ego. The ego will never be fulfilled! The ego always wants more. If you strive to please the ego, your fulfillment will be fleeting, as it will keep you searching for the next thing to fulfill you. It also leads to a "victim" mentality that blames other people and circumstances on why you aren't happy. However, being fulfilled is your responsibility and you are the captain of your ship! You can experience fulfillment regardless of your past circumstance.

If you've read my book, "Divine Worth," you know that I struggled with self worth issues most of my life. In order to feel like I was good enough, I pushed myself to succeed. When I finally reached society's success model and had the career, the house, the car, and the bank account, I realized I wasn't happy. I couldn't understand why I felt so unfulfilled because I was doing everything I was "supposed" to do! To make things worse, I used cigarettes and alcohol to try and avoid the voice within me that was telling me that there's more to life than living up to society's success model.

I finally answered that higher calling, that voice within, and realized how to truly feel fulfilled.

Key Insight #4: True fulfillment is achieved by aligning your core purpose with a means of serving with joy.

While your ego seeks to gain, your divine essence (a.k.a., soul or spirit) seeks to be of service in the world. Your divine essence doesn't need to gain anything, because the rewards of serving from a place of joy and purpose creates fulfillment within itself.

If you are a heart-centered, purpose-driven person, you probably know what I mean, and also experience:

- A desire to share something with the world and make a positive impact (even if you aren't completely sure what it is).
- A sense of higher calling within you (and a sense of anxiety and lack of fulfillment when you don't follow it or can't hear it clearly).

- An extreme sense of joy and fulfillment when you do align with your core purpose and share your gifts.

So, why don't people realize and shift out of these misconceptions?

Key Insight #5: Four main reasons people stay stuck in the misconceptions that block them:

They aren't aware of their disempowering beliefs. As I mentioned, many of us are conditioned to believe these things in our society, and we have a human need to be accepted. But look at how many people suffer from anxiety, addiction and depression! It takes courage to follow your heart and blaze your own path.

1. **Fear.** Whether it is a fear of not having enough, or not being good enough, fear can keep you stuck in your comfort zone and feeling disempowered.

2. **Lack of clarity about your purpose.** If you aren't clear about what your divine and core purposes are, you may feel lost, as if you're floating through life with no sense of direction.

3. **Lack of action.** It's one thing to know your purpose, but it's another to take action on fulfilling it. Remember I mentioned earlier that your purpose is a verb, and a verb means action. Once you know your purpose, it's time to take action on fulfilling it so you can experience and create!

It is my passion to help you overcome what keeps you stuck so you can connect with and fulfill your purpose. One way I do this is to help you discover what your purpose is, and then start and grow a business that is aligned with it, so that you can help people and experience freedom, fulfillment and abundance.

Bonnie Wirth

Bonnie Wirth, Universal Empowerment Facilitator is often referred to as the "Ultimate SOUL Coach." She is an inspirational speaker, sought after self-empowerment consultant, co-facilitator of the "Experience Yourself" Women's Retreats, and Editor-in-Chief of PUREOne Magazine. Bonnie's passion for helping others comes as a result of her own personal life experiences which inspire and support her commitment in raising consciousness while assisting people to initiate healing within and embrace their truth and life with authenticity, passion and appreciation.

Location: Lloydminster, SK Canada

www.bonniewirth.net

www.pureonemagazine.com

www.experienceyourself.net

✉ **purebybonnie@gmail.com**

f **facebook.com/pages/PURE-By-Bonnie/109224275811197**

f **facebook.com/puremagazinebybonnie**

f **facebook.com/experienceyourself**

🐦 **@Bonnie_Wirth**

LESSON 4

SOUL INSPIRED

By Bonnie Wirth

Knowing who you are is imperative for change of any kind. You have to know what you desire, what you like and do not like, what you want more of and what you would love to experience differently. The moment you begin to question any aspect of your life is the moment you actually open the door for change to begin.

Knowing who you are inside is everything for change to happen rapidly! The simplest of truths is that no matter what you think about you or consider possible, how it is that you see yourself or believe and define yourself to be at the core, you are SOUL. Your divine nature makes all things possible!

Change is a funny thing. It can make us feel uneasy; it can also be very exciting! Imagine a world where nothing changed. It would be a boring and monotonous existence. Change happens constantly, inviting us to step out of our comfort zones, take chances to manifest dreams into reality and create miracles for our life. Dreams come true when we initiate and follow through with changes by listening to the guidance of our heart.

Now, sometimes more often than not, change shakes us up. We get uncomfortable and fearful of the unknown, causing us to avoid, push against and resist it. We actually make this process much harder on ourselves than what it needs to be. Change IS always good! "Good is simply GOD with two O's."

I am an "everything happens for a reason greater than me" kind of girl, since change has always brought something amazing into my life even though at the time it felt out of control and had me a bit off balance and faltering in Faith. Depending on the circumstances, admittedly there were times when I got angry, blamed other people and felt completely helpless; and yes, in those moments I was rolling around on the floor crying, "Why me?" Big changes also had me coming up with excuses, reasons and alibis to support the choice to run the other direction.

This is something most people find themselves going through at one time or another especially when the changes are life-altering and unexpected, and it's totally fine. It's not "good" or "bad." It's called being human.

I was a huge procrastinator; putting off change or taking as long as possible to make a decision. I had a tendency to ask other people for their opinions too, swayed by what seemed to be logical explanations and reasoning as to why they thought I should not take the chance. I obviously valued other people's opinions more than I valued my own. I was afraid of getting it wrong, making mistakes, failing and not being liked.

I recognize now how many times I gave away my power to others when I allowed them to decide what was best for me. By doing so, I diminished my voice of reason, allowed fear to grow and felt completely blocked.

Time to upgrade my belief systems! They were interrupting my ability to welcome change.

- I could not be trusted to make good decisions
- I am a failure, a fraud, stupid…
- I am not worthy and deserving of love, success, abundance, freedom…
- I am not good enough

The Course in Miracles states, "There is no cause for Faithlessness but there is always Cause for Faith." I often remind myself to go with the flow; Let Go and Let God and have Faith the Universe will carry me. Having Faith in me is not always easy.

Faith is empowering. I can choose to rely on my ego to talk me out of moving forward or I can choose to listen to the inspiration of my soul to provide me with the appropriate action steps necessary to take me from where I am to where I desire to be. Change is inevitable, so my job is to learn how to navigate easily through it.

We need to heal limiting belief systems and release ourselves from a consciousness that no longer serves. We cannot move forward in the direction of our dreams and make positive changes when we are still hanging onto resentments and grudges and not willing to forgive ourselves or others.

As vibrational beings, the Universe responds vibrationally to us. Simply put, we get what we give! Unconscious and conscious requests are flying out into the Universe with every thought and feeling we have. This is why it is important to pay attention to what we are ordering from the life experience catalogue!

We are the creators of reality, and our habits of thought, whether positive or negative and the crap we are hanging onto from the past, all create cellular and energetic patterning. This greatly influences our state of being, our ability to make rapid change and our results.

Our heart-mind also holds beliefs at the soul level which may not be serving us either.

- I am a disappointment to God
- I am dishonoring God by my choices
- I fear God

It becomes equally important to clean up our vibrations and to shift and heal limitations on all levels of our being in order to live a happy and fulfilled life. The reward in doing this allows change to flow effortlessly.

SOUL is a divine catalyst for positive, personal transformation. She calls out, guiding, nudging and gently moving us along, always. There is constant movement forward, whether we are aware of it or not. She guides every decision even when we have logically thought it through; higher self has assisted in the decision. This is the reason we can never make the wrong choice.

Our divine nature is love. Centering decisions from love and following our inner guidance always serves. It is good for us, our family and our finances too.

What IF change could be easy? Well, it can be! With love, "Get out of your way!"

I personally find it very helpful to:

- Shut off outside influences. This ensures that no one else's opinions are interfering with what feels right.
- Keep guidance sacred. There will always be someone who does not understand, or who will say it is not possible. I am less likely to give up when no one else's energy or opinion is interrupting.
- Detach from negative people in order to maintain a high vibration while I am working on becoming the best version of me.
- Honor myself. Make choices which serve, including nutrition, exercise, yoga and meditation. This makes it easier to live from my heart center.

A few things I know for sure:

Change is a "Call to Action" from SOUL. You have been praying for help, asking for more in your life by setting goals and getting clear on intentions. Spirit always knows exactly what needs to shift and heal within so you receive the answer to your prayers, to grow and expand within consciousness. She calls in the change in response to receiving more and living your purpose.

Remain Heart-Centered when making decisions. Stay focused on living from the heart versus the conscious mind. Taking time to get quiet and fall into your heart unlocks inner wisdom for the best advice possible. You will feel calmer and more peaceful during times of big change, too.

Seek Alignment. Stay connected and grounded with Source, your higher self and God. Do whatever you need to do to feel good and stay positive through thoughts, feelings, actions and reactions. The higher self is the eternal consciousness. Living in alignment creates an energetic vibrational parallel between the Universe and your heart. When you feel good, it is easy for all you have been praying for to show up. Change flows.

Take a deep breath and notice something beautiful around you when feeling anxious. Remaining centered and calm allows for ease through transitions almost effortlessly as the universe works its magic.

You are greater than all your struggles, troubles and woes. Life happens for your evolvement. SOUL is supporting and loving you through it all. You are here to grow, learn and achieve Joy; experiences, through change, are leading you there. Trust that what is happening "to" you is happening "for" you.

You are Infinite Energy. Everything is energy. Vibrating, moving, shifting and rearranging in accordance to Universal Laws. Your thoughts and feelings shape the world around you. You have the power to make change in a heartbeat.

Your Soul is your greatest resource, infinite wisdom and love! She illuminates the power of choices that are in alignment with your greatest ambitions and provides guidance to successfully achieve. Inspiration and action from within assures you will never make the wrong decision, and any change, big or small of any kind will be good!

So, my friends, follow the inspiration of your Soul. Trust that when you do, you will be well taken care of. Relax, have some fun and embrace change like never before!

Karla Kadlec

Karla Kadlec awakens the heart's wisdom with consciousness medicine. As a BodyTalk Practitioner, she resolves conflict within the bodymind by focusing on the whole person for whole healthcare. Karla helps people to unlock and access their innate wisdom, enabling each heart to become its own sage. As a BodyTalk Instructor, Karla supports new practitioners in developing their structured intuition and efficiently facilitate profound healing for their own clients. Her authentic communication style is a beacon of encouragement for others to explore and tap into their own body wisdom. Karla helps people "get on with it" so they can "do the thing."

Vancouver, Canada

www.sageheart.ca

1 (604) 603 1641

karla@sageheart.ca

facebook.com/SageHeartHealingArts

youtube.com/SageHeartHealingArts

linkedin.com/in/karlakadlec

AN OPEN HEART IS AN INSPIRED HEART

By Karla Kadlec

"Letting go gives us freedom, and freedom is the only condition for happiness. If in our heart, we still cling to anything – anger, anxiety or possessions – we cannot be free."

~ Thich Nhat Hanh

When I was a teenager I suffered a lot. I suffered because I pretended that what others thought of me didn't matter, but actually it hurt me incredibly. I stuffed my hurt into my body and blamed others for the misery I felt. I never allowed myself the opportunity to process my emotions because I believed emotions were a sign of weakness. My body developed fibromyalgia, sleeping problems and a bad attitude. When I went to a western medicine specialist at 17 years old about the pain in my body she told me to "get used to it." Hearing this statement propelled me into alternative forms of healing and medicine. I was not willing to "get used to" pain and suffering.

I healed my body by taking personal responsibility for my behaviors, emotions and life. When I began studying BodyTalk in 2005 I knew I had found the modality I was looking for, because it's designed to work in harmony with an individual's own healing capacity and innate wisdom. I also knew it was too incredible not to be shared, so I started teaching and sharing my understanding with others by opening my business Sage Heart Healing Arts.

When we feel like we're lost and have no direction, we tend to look outside of ourselves for the answers. We look to friends or family to give us direction. The joke is on us, however, because that beautiful, beating heart inside our chest actually generates instructions and directions related to our soul's path. When your heart is open, it's easy to listen to the whisper of the heart. When it's closed, in lock-down mode, its messages are blocked from getting through, and so we look to the external for answers. Let me tell you, if you do not listen to the whisper of the heart, you will eventually get a frying pan to the face. My frying pan was my illness as a teen, for others it can be a breakup or a car crash. That's the moment the universe turns your world upside down to let you know something needs to change, and fast!

A client shared with me that her life felt dull, she was unmotivated and stuck. She wanted to live a life of inspiration and vibrancy, but it felt far away from her. We started our BodyTalk session in the typical way; she relaxed on the massage table and I contacted her right hand. By connecting with innate wisdom using the BodyTalk Protocol, healing priorities for Clara were revealed.

BODYTALK AGENDA: OPEN THE HEART INTO SELF

The information I gathered through Clara's session indicated that she needed repair on a cellular level relating to her self-perspective. Her view of herself had become skewed; she was listening to the opinions of others more than listening to her own heart. We corrected this pattern on a cellular level so future cells that are created could hold this improved consciousness related to "Self." Next we focused on the Fire Element with the consciousness of the "I am." By strengthening the Fire Element within Clara she would be able to feel the inspirational light from within more readily.

Then we created and declared the permission statement, "I give my heart permission to open," and Clara recognized that she was the one that cut her heart off from the world. This heart disconnection served as a protective mechanism at one point, but because it was no longer serving her, she let it go.

Next, an Active Memory came up for healing, related to the Fear of Ridicule. She experienced deep anxiety that what she shared with others would become a target for negativity and attack. The last part was to bring circulation, repair and introspection to the right atrium of the heart, the location of her soul.

In the days and weeks that followed, Clara reported that her life was moving forward and she was enjoying many changes. By confronting the fears she had felt in the past, she was able to free herself up, thus making her available for what the universe had in store.

Clara's story is not unique. I meet many smart and savvy women in my practice, and they often suffer from what I call Stuck Spirit Syndrome. For some it manifests by weakening their drive to reach for their goals and dreams. For others it is a state of disempowerment that is so thick, they have forgotten that they are in charge of their lives. Even worse, some women believe their lives here on this planet are a mistake. Something "out there" made a mistake and they aren't supposed to be alive. What!? That is totally closed-heart thinking and we have to dispel those notions right now. You are here. That is proof alone that you deserve to live life. What kind of life you deserve to live is up to YOU!

YES, IT'S UP TO YOU!

When you feel funky, sucky, pouty, stuck, and full of despair, it is a sure sign that you are in a spiritual starvation mode. You have cut yourself off from your heart and therefore from your spirit. Have you booked a pity party table for one? If so, here's what you need to do:

1. First set a time limit for this state of mind! How long do you want to feel this way? How long can you afford to feel this way? Another 3 minutes, 3 days or 3 months? The time is up to you, so pick a time.

2. Then amp up your pity party. Make it ridiculous. Notice yourself in this pathetic state, observe yourself moaning, complaining, blaming, victimizing and belittling yourself. Get it out of your system. Feel it to the bottom. You'll know you've felt it to the bottom when you get to the end of your sorrow. Some people don't allow themselves enough time at the pity party to actually let go of the feeling. Feel it all so you can learn, process the experience and gain wisdom in your heart.

3. Feeling it to the bottom is like sinking in a dark swimming pool; you're struggling, you can't breathe, you're panicked

and you're scared… But every pool has a bottom and you can hit the bottom of a feeling, then PUSH yourself back up to the light.

WHAT LETTING IT GO REALLY MEANS

Letting something go really means having no emotional charge around it anymore. If you have ended a relationship where your heart experienced heartbreak, you may want the other party to know they have wronged you, hurt you, and are at fault. That's a story. Drop it. "But I just want them to know what they're missing!" Drop it! The longer you hold onto this story of wanting the impossible from the other person – the longer you hold that frequency in your energy field – the longer your heart stays closed to new experiences.

Some sage advice to help you go from spiritless to inspired.

1. **Return to Balance**. One cannot "stay balanced." This sounds like you can hold on to a moment in time, which you cannot. You do have the choice to return to balance within each moment. A BodyTalk Session shines a light on the areas that need to shift back into balance.

2. **Know yourself**. Before you can fully accept yourself, you must really recognize your beliefs, behaviors and patterns. Having a behavior you don't like doesn't mean you are unlikable, just human. Take responsibility for your behaviors. Make self-inquiry a fun act of curiosity.

3. **Let go of blame**. When you engage in conflict with yourself or with others your mind wants to blame "someone" for the discomfort. Recognize that the feelings within you are yours. No one "makes you feel."

4. **Let emotions flow**. Anger moves. Fear activates. Worry thinks. Grief dissipates. Sadness evaluates. If you only allow certain emotions to be expressed, you deny yourself the full emotional palette. Emotions express your energy. Do not deny the energy channels; blocked emotions block the wisdom of the heart.

5.   **Be Grateful**. Shift your focus to what is working, and what has always been working for you. Say thank you to the universe for this abundance showing up in your life. Breathe it into every cell in your body. Notice where you have limits to your gratitude. This is where you can work to shift limiting beliefs.

6.   **Be vulnerable with your creativity**. To live from the heart means that you agree to express your unique perspective with the world. Creativity comes in many forms; discover the language your heart wants to speak and share your gifts with the world.

One of the greatest lessons I learned in this life is that an open heart protects me, a closed heart limits me. An open heart can neutralize any negative energy coming towards it. An open heart invites other hearts to open, therefore my open heart serves not only me but all those around me. Will you open your sage heart to inspiration, love and joy?

Rochele Lawson

Rochele Lawson is a Registered Nurse, Ayurvedic Health Practitioner, Holistic Health and Wellness Consultant, Best Selling Author and Speaker. She is President of The Health, Healing & Wellness Company, founded to bring holistic health and wellness into the lives of individuals seeking a natural path to wellness. Rochele's energy, guidance and enthusiasm have helped thousands of people improve their health and well-being, holistically and naturally. Rochele is the author of "Intro to Holistic Health, Ayurveda Style," a guest writer for Supermomceo.com blog and has her own weekly syndicated radio show, "Blissful Living." Rochele has spent over 20 years assisting people to achieve optimal health and wellness so that they can live the life of their dreams.

www.stressassessmentmagic.com

✉ **rochele@rochelelawson.com**

🅕 **facebook.com/rochele.lawson**

🅣 **twitter.com/rochelelawson**

▶ **youtube.com/user/rochelelawson**

🅘 **linkedin.com/rochelelawson**

BLISSFUL WISDOM: USING YOUR INNER WISDOM FOR SUCCESS WITH YOUR WELL-BEING

By Rochele Lawson

An internal guidance system is something that we are all born with and have the natural ability to access. Some people acknowledge their internal guidance system and access it often to assist them with their daily life. Then there are those individuals that believe they may have an internal guidance system but don't know how to access it and lastly, there are those individuals that don't believe in an "internal guidance system," at all. I want you to know that everyone has an internal guidance system. It is often referred to as "intuition." This internal guidance system is with us from the moment we are born until the moment we die. In fact, once that first breath is taken, our internal guidance system is switched on. I refer to my internal guidance system, as my personal GPS that allows me to access my "Blissful Wisdom," at any time. "Blissful Wisdom" goes beyond the use of your intuition; it is actually your connection to the divine spirit that resides within you, and it is yours to use for everything you want to do or achieve in life.

My relationship with "Blissful Wisdom" began when I was a little girl. My grandmother used to say that I was a very intuitive little girl and that one day my intuition was going to help me to help a lot of people. I would know things about myself and other people without knowing how I knew them or how I obtained the information. I would share this information with my grandmother and she would say, "When you receive information about other people, it is best not to share it with them, not unless you are asked for the information. This is so you don't frighten people, however for you, it is very important that you listen to the guidance within you because it will never lead you astray." She would call this internal guidance "Blissful Wisdom." I remember her saying, "It will lead you to a life of bliss when you learn to follow its guidance." My grandma often discussed with me how "Blissful Wisdom" was something that was always available to me and that I had access to use it, anytime I wanted for all purposes in life.

As I grew up, I listened and tested the use of my "Blissful Wisdom." Sometimes I listened very well and sometimes I didn't listen at all. It was the times that I failed to listen to this guidance, that were the most challenging times in my life. Not listening to my "Blissful Wisdom" led me to experience one of the most challenging times in my life. That time was so excoriatingly difficult that once I persevered through the challenge, I vowed to always follow the internal guidance bestowed upon me, in all areas of my life. By following my "Blissful Wisdom," I was able to heal myself from a medical condition, holistically and naturally, in 9 months after suffering with the condition for 17 years. I used "Blissful Wisdom" to assist me with the care of my patients when I worked as a Registered Nurse in the Emergency Department, and I've used it to guide me to being a successful entrepreneur for the last 24 years.

Naturally, I wanted to share this technique with others so I incorporated it in a process that allowed me to include the principles of Ayurveda to deepen the process for sustainable results. I was guided to share this with my clients. My clients began to experience amazing, significant and sustainable improvements to their health and wellbeing.

As an Ayurvedic Health Practitioner, incorporating the spirit in well-being is part of what I do. Ayurveda is a holistic medical modality that originated in India between 3,500 – 5,000 years ago. It focuses on harmony and balance of the mind, body and spirit. "Blissful Wisdom" falls into the category of "Spirit." Holistic medicine takes into account that the spirit is involved in the health and well-being of the mind and the body. All three of these individual components work together in synchronicity to bring harmony and balance to each other.

45

Using the wisdom of your "spirit," your "internal guidance system," or simply your "Blissful Wisdom," can assist you in successfully managing your health and well-being. It is a key ingredient to shining light on any road blocks or challenges that prevent you from having the energy, vibrancy, clarity, confidence and feeling of well-being that you desire. This wisdom guides you to unique solutions designed to help you successfully overcome challenges and road blocks.

Everyone is born with an inner guidance system or "Blissful Wisdom," and it is available to use at anytime. The process of accessing this wisdom is very simple to do, yet your ego is designed to lead you to believe that this inner guidance is "make believe" or false information but rest assured that the information is correct and very accurate. In fact, the wisdom of the information that you receive is so unique to you and your challenges that you can't fail, if you follow its guidance. It's this inner wisdom that leads you to higher levels of consciousness, designed to provide you solutions that create rapid, positive changes in your physical body and skill in healing yourself.

The first major challenge that I engaged in using my "Blissful Wisdom" was to heal myself of the medical condition that plagued me for 17 years. I was initially guided to use the technique that I now call the "Quiet Time Technique." It literally involved me taking time out to get quiet. Here's how it works. Start by setting aside 5 minutes a day to do this. I suggest making this an appointment in your calendar. Then gradually increase the time to no more than 30 minutes. Sit in an area where you will not be disturbed, turn down or off any electronic devices, (there were no cell phones or IPad or computers when I began using this technique). In the beginning, just sit quietly and let the thoughts flow in and out of your mind.

As you become more comfortable with the "Quiet Time Technique," you can begin each session with a question about your well-being that you would like answered. You can use this technique to get guidance on all aspects of your life, however since your health is the greatest wealth that you posses, I'm choosing to focus upon it. As you engage in the "Quiet Time Technique" with the question in your mind, sit quietly and allow the thoughts to flow in. These thoughts will be the guidance to your question. I suggest beginning with one question;

as you lengthen the time of your session, then you can engage in the process of asking a question, getting the guidance and asking the next question. Limit your session to no more than 30 minutes. You will know the session has come to an end when the guidance stops flowing in pertaining to the question. Please note that "Quiet Time Technique" is not a meditation, however you can use it as your meditative process. It is a powerful process of using the quietness of your mind to fully engage in dialogue with your "Blissful Wisdom." I would equate it to having a very deep conversation with someone that knows you better than anyone else; and that someone is your Divine, "Blissful" Self.

The "Quiet Time Technique" is a great way to start learning how to access your inner wisdom for guidance with your health and well-being. The accuracy, success and benefits that I received from using this technique and sharing it with my clients, allows me to successfully engage them in the spirit process of mind, body, spirit healing. As you grow more comfortable with using "Blissful Wisdom" for guidance in your health and well-being, you will increasingly understand the magnificence of this gift that the Divine has bestowed upon all of us.

"Blissful Wisdom" gives you the tools and techniques to make every day of your life full of energy, harmony, clarity, vibrancy and love. Learning how to access and use "Blissful Wisdom" assists you with taking that giant step forward to optimal health and well-being. If you are ready to take that giant step forward towards a more balanced, healthy, calm and connected life, then I invite you to start with the "Quiet Time Technique." Developing confidence with "Blissful Wisdom" is similar to personal growth, with one major difference; when you use "Blissful Wisdom" you're connecting to the Divine source and using that connection to empower yourself to improve your health, your well-being and your life.

Many people go through life spending time, energy and money worrying about why what they do to improve their health and well-being doesn't work. They go through life trying this or that with no sustainable success and eventually feel despondent and defeated. I want you to stop struggling to obtain the health and well-being that you deserve and desire. I invite you to take that first step towards improved health and wellness by engaging in the "Quiet Time Technique." When you're ready to go deep with rapid success and personalized guidance, I invite you to connect with me. It's far easier to travel the path to Optimal Health and Wellbeing with someone walking beside you giving you personalized guidance.

What are you waiting for?

Kaayla Vedder

Kaayla Vedder has spent more than two decades honing her skills as an intuitive energy healer, so clients in Canada and around the world can live healthier lives free of density and full of joy. Able to see energy since childhood, Kaayla has developed a system for tapping into the dance of divine energy, bridging the gap between humanity and our higher levels so people can release what no longer serves them. The results are astounding.

To find out more about how Kaayla can help you move towards better health and live in the fluidity of divine grace, please visit her website at **http://kripaquantumhealing.com/**.

To book an appointment with her immediately, email her at **kaayla@ kripaquantumhealing.com**

f **facebook.com/KripaQuantumHealing**

in **linkedin.com/pub/kaayla-vedder/62/a4b/84**

LESSON 7

WHAT YOU FOCUS ON EXPANDS

By Kaayla Vedder

When I started my energy healing practice more than 20 years ago, I had no idea how important my work was going to become – or how long it was going to take our medical system to stop merely eliminating the symptoms of poor health and start liberating Vitality. While there are many aspects to the magic I weave through my business, Kripa Quantum Healing, a lot of it occurs in three main areas: beliefs, telomeric breathing and fractals. The words may sound strange but they actually refer to concepts that are simple enough for a five-year-old to understand!

And although many people think that the health we have is the health we're stuck with, there **is** another answer; healing our bodies is actually as easy as paying attention to them and releasing the negative energy that has been holding us hostage from within – the negative beliefs about our attractiveness, the sorrow over how we were parented, the trauma of an accident... What if those perceptively bad experiences left a legacy of negative energy that permeated our hearts and minds and somehow got trapped in our bodies to fester and infect our health?

What if there were a way to transmute that negative energy into something light, airy, joyful and healthy?

Although I've been seeing energy for as long as I can remember, I didn't do much with it for an awfully long time. Like most people, I was caught up in the scramble to make a living, build a family and stay balanced in the best way I could. After my marriage fell apart, I became a single mom earning a great income with a fantastic job in corporate sales. In time I took a bigger job with another company and soon thereafter I began experiencing symptoms that were consistent with a serious illness. My new employer merged with another big company… and I was out on my ear.

It was a humbling time in my life, a phase I now recognize as an opportunity for the "Cosmic Reset" that allowed me to evaluate what I was doing with my life. I hounded the western medical system for a resolution to my health issues but no one could figure out what was wrong with me, let alone cure me. Was I condemned to a short future full of illness and pain? How was I going to raise my children? How could I possibly earn an income? I turned in desperation to a combination of homeopathic medicine and energy healing and I never once looked back.

With consistent application of specific healing principles and techniques I brought myself back to full glowing health. I began to study different "alternative" healing modalities and filled an entire wall with certificates proclaiming my proficiency in them. I began helping other people rediscover full health for themselves.

It was rewarding work and I felt proud of my ability to follow protocols and obtain amazing results for people. Eventually I began to wonder if there were an even simpler way to promote health. Energy behaves according to scientific principles that some of the most brilliant minds on the planet have identified and codified. What if healing were actually just about moving energy?

Extensive research into this question has shown me that our beliefs are crucial to our health. Scientific experiments have shown that our expectations affect our results, so if you change your expectations, you change your results. And what you focus on expands.

We've all heard that some of us are genetically predisposed to developing health issues such as heart disease, cancer, cellulite and alcoholism. If a number of your relatives have experienced breast cancer, for example, you might believe that it's "in the family." But if that's true, why doesn't every woman in your family get it? The conclusion many brilliant people have come to is that even if you have the genetic coding for a disease it will not manifest unless it is activated by a specific protein that your body generates in response to an emotional trigger. And what causes your emotions? Your beliefs!

Part of my practice now involves working with people to transform their beliefs about themselves and their health so that they, too, can focus on and enjoy vibrant, glowing health. In fact, I've developed a strong expertise in transmuting people's limiting beliefs so their life shows up differently for them. This releases them from the past and helps them luxuriate in the unconditional love of our Creator.

Another part of what I do for people lies in teaching them to breathe telomerically. That's a fancy word for learning to breathe in harmony with all that Is. Your body is in constant communication with everything around you – you send and receive information along a highly sophisticated built-in radio frequency that is continuously communicating with your environment. This "scanning system" is always on, always available, and always correct. And it operates through more than 70 trillion tiny receptors called telomeres that are located on every cell in your body. The more you aware are of and acknowledge their existence, the more effective they are.

It sounds bizarre, and when I first heard about telomeres I thought, "Whaaaaaat?" Even TV medical celebrity Dr. Oz talks about telomeres, though, and after I began investigating, I incorporated telomeric breathing into my practice. It's a game-changer. I now teach my clients to breathe telomerically and if you do this one thing once a day for 30 days, your life will change beyond anything you can imagine. This is not something you should do while driving, and it is particularly satisfying when done outside, in Nature. Here's an abbreviated lesson in what to do:

Step One: Find a quiet place, close your eyes, and take a couple of deep belly breaths, expanding your belly all the way out.

Step Two: Imagine that every single cell in your body is breathing in and out with you and that there are amazing white packages of unconditionally loving light flowing through your body with every breath you take. Imagine that you are drawing that light down through the top of your head and that you are visiting every part of your body on a journey down to the bottom of your feet.

Step Three: Imagine, also, as you breathe, that there is a shower just above you and that a rain of beautiful white light is spraying the light all the way down through your body and out the bottom of your feet, ridding you of all the gray, all the density.

Step Three: Release, exhaling. You may experience emotions or old beliefs that are no longer serving you as they come up to leave. If you're tired sleep, if you're hungry, eat.

I'm afraid I can't explain telomeric breathing using mathematical principles and scientific formulas, but I take comfort from the fact that in a world that has been overrun with math and science, there are still inexplicable things that make our hearts beat faster and our spirits fly higher. We need to focus on them, too.

There is a place for both science and magic in our world, and fractals seem to be an area where the two unite. Fractals are patterns where the smaller part of an object perfectly reflects the whole. Scientists use them to describe phenomena that appear random or chaotic, such as crystal growth and galaxy formation. But here's the interesting thing: **when you change one part of a fractal pattern, the entire system reorganizes itself to incorporate the change.** Remember when we talked earlier about changing your underlying beliefs? Well, not only will that immediately tell your body that things are different, but you will fractally integrate the change so that not only is it part of what you now believe, it is part of who you actually are. And who those around us are, as well. We are all fractally connected, and we are more similar than we are different. With fractals, we can move beyond the density of the reality we believe is real.

So what can you do to expand greater health and vitality? It's amazingly simple:

1. Transmute any limiting beliefs you have about yourself, your life, your past and your future.

2. Practice telomeric breathing and receive Divine Love in every cell of your body.

3. Trust that your health is fractally related to your beliefs. Your willingness to release your history and step into your destiny will help reveal the true essence of who you were meant to be.

People typically show up at my door after they've tried everything else. They are desperate and in pain. We talk about what's presenting in their lives and I use my skills as an energy healer to help them tune in to their natural frequency of boisterous good health. We need fabulous energy! And, sometimes, we need a little help generating it. I am privileged to be able to provide that assistance.

Fiona Mayhill

Fiona is a Certified BodyTalk Practitioner. The BodyTalk System™ is a body-mind therapy that finds the underlying causes of illness by addressing the whole-person and their whole-story. Fiona is also a teacher, mentor, and facilitator of courses on sexuality and relationships. She is owner of Innerlife Health Services, a holistic health clinic located in Victoria, BC Canada.

Working with Fiona shines a light on areas of health, sexuality and life where we feel stuck or limited. Her work gently transforms these places we feel wounded into reasons for celebration.

Work with Fiona through her clinic, via phone/Skype or join one of her classes.

innerlife.ca

- **(1) 250-415-8566**
- **fiona_mayhill**
- **fiona@innerlife.ca, innerlifehealth@gmail.com**
- **facebook.com/pages/Innerlife-Health-Services/221740174508979**

LESSON 8

SEXUAL INTIMACY: DANCING WITH OUR DARK SIDE

By Fiona Mayhill

"And those who were seen dancing were thought to be insane
by those who could not hear the music."

~ Nietzsche

I love all the awkward and terrifying intimate moments in bed with a lover. The weird musky smells, the hair from somewhere that ends up in my mouth, and the farting sounds of wet bellies coming together and pulling apart. I love the insecurity of wondering how jiggly and wrinkly I look, how bad my breath smells and if my leg hair is sharp enough to pill the bed sheets. I love the embarrassment I feel when one of us gets turned off. I love when I'm disgusted by his noises and irritated by him rubbing the wrong spot for far too long, the guilt I imagine he feels when I tell him, and the shame I feel if I don't. And I love the sharp rejection and aching loneliness I feel when he disconnects after connection.

I also love all the comfortable and fun intimate parts too, but those have always been easier to love.

For most of my life, I didn't love any of what I think of as my darkness: intense emotions, feelings and sensations. I judged them and rejected whatever put me in touch with them. I had surmised that emotionally mature meant controlled and fairly emotionless. I thought the goal of life was to "let go of" (interpreted as "get rid of") uncomfortable feelings. Ironically, this suppression and elimination approach just sent my unwelcome parts underground where they eroded and distorted my relationship with my body and my life.

Many of us have been taught some form of a tightly controlled waltz, but inside we are dying to tango. We express ourselves in varying degrees through our instinctual, emotional body: sensation, emotion, sound and movement. However, only a narrow bandwidth of expression feels comfortable or safe (the waltz). The uncomfortable feelings on either side of the safe zone lurk in the shadows, producing manipulative relationships with anything that brings these feelings to light.

What if I told you that feeling the full spectrum of all that is dark, from the slightly uncomfortable to the downright excruciating, is the path to deeper love, ecstasy and sexual fulfillment?

When I open or close to my darkness – pleasure, anger, desire, fear, grief, shame, guilt – I feel like I'm being danced. The sensations and emotions fill my body, like I'm being pulled onto the dance floor by a sexy Latin lover and lost in the gyrating movement of hips. My sexuality, my spiritual essence is magnetized and moved by the sensual nature of what lies beneath the surface of all that is physical. What I have learned is that my dark side is a gift, and she makes an excellent dance partner.

This wasn't always the case. I didn't know I had rejected my darkness and cocooned myself into numbness through my childhood and adolescence. I just thought I was innately flawed. I thought the world around me was pretty dysfunctional too.

I became a teacher, I believed, so that I could enlighten everyone and reduce suffering in the world. But trying to solve suffering through intellectual deconstruction and discussion never resulted in relief. "Let's talk about" always spun tighter and stickier webs. My need for freedom from this controlling, self-sabotaging approach became the impetus behind becoming a health practitioner. So I was really ready for the powerful insight that came from a particularly challenging time in my life and taught me to dance with the dark.

I had pushed beyond my edge at a workshop, ended my marriage and was dumped by my lover. And then I lost my voice. For two and a half months all that would issue from my throat was a small hissing sound. This was accompanied by a crippling depression, loss of appetite, inability to sleep and heart heaviness so intense I sometimes couldn't breathe or move. There was no way to distract myself from my suffering. I felt alone. The dark swallowed me up and I let it.

In that stillness, silence and depth of my surrender, I came to life. I realized that I always thought and talked, but never actually listened... really listened with my whole body. Thinking and talking and analyzing had convinced me I was really getting somewhere. But in fact, the intellectualization and endless discussion actually disconnected me from an infinitely erotic landscape of sensations.

Every one of my senses came alive and I started realizing how afraid I was to feel. And see. And hear. And taste. And smell. By listening with my whole body I found freedom from fear. I literally went out of my mind... and came back to my senses.

My body, which had previously felt like a needy, demanding burden became an exotic, mysterious land. My shameful dark corners, once feared and disowned, now were sources of curiosity and delight. Since then, I have loved discovering dark parts in me that want to dance. It is so deliciously uncomfortable.

Our dark side triggers vulnerability, which we instinctively want to brace against, push through or move away from. This defensiveness creates habituated patterns of rejection, isolation, and numbness that feed on chronic hidden fears driving addictions and dis-ease in the body and mind. The irony is that by avoiding our dark side, we feel worse.

It is impossible to begin intimately dancing with your dark side until you know how she is revealing herself to you. If she has patterned herself deeply in your body, she may look like physical health issues. She may also look like anxiety, depression or conflict in relationships and sexual intimacy issues. Wherever you find suffering, know that she is there.

Leaning into discomfort and darkness runs counter to our instinct for safety and our preference for comfort. Going into the dark with our whole body reconnects us, helps us see wholeness in our flaws and transforms our fears into love. From years of working with my own darkness, I appreciate the need for support, therapy and practices that help us open up, lean in and dance. It is my greatest passion to help others embrace their darkness and remember their erotic sensual and sexual nature. Let's not just shuffle through the waltz but tango our hearts wide open.

Getting into bed with someone always provides us with opportunities to dance with our dark side. If it's a good relationship, it will likely feel awful too. The bright light of orgasmic bliss, even just the dream of it, backlights our suffering. This is why sex is simultaneously so alluring and terrifying. Our fears of imperfection and performance are actually invitations to dance, maybe even dirty dance. That's good sex, not just in bed but also in life.

Do you want to deepen your sexual intimacy right now?

- Your sexual spiritual essence is alive in you right now. How full is your breath? How open is your body? How open or closed you are right now reflects the degree to which you are experiencing yourself sexually. Take a deep breath in and breathe out fully. You just became sexier. And deepened your intimacy.

- All emotions are incredibly erotic. Nothing is as sensual as the fiery, scalding flare of anger, the smoldering sting of jealousy, or the hot flush of shame. MMMMmmmm... Can you feel your body squirm right now at the thought of these feelings? Instead of clamping down your breath, open it up. Feel more of the sensations. Breathe more deeply. Allow your body to move, even just a little.

- Notice that right now you are alone. Even if you are in a busy room full of people, only you can hear your thoughts, see what you see, smell what you smell, feel what you feel. Sensing is an inward turning. It's a personal journey. Really hate it. And then really enjoy it. Notice how delicious that contrast feels.

- Open your body slowly and intentionally right now. Lift your arms above your head. Spread your legs. Gently arch your back and push your chest out, not for the sake of achieving anything but to enjoy the sensual and emotional rollercoaster. Notice any self-consciousness. Resistance. Refusal. Bliss. Feel it all with your whole body.

- We are as quick to try to shut down our pleasure as we are our pain. Have you ever been paid a compliment and noticed the rush of intense sensations that fill your body? They are so pleasurable they are almost painful. Compliment yourself right now. Feel it. Then criticize yourself. Feel it. Both offer us sensual orgasms.

- The very next time you open your mouth to speak, notice if you can feel first.

- And now, if you want more intimate sex in the bedroom, do all of the above the next time you're in bed, with or without someone else.

Rapid Results Whole Self Wheel

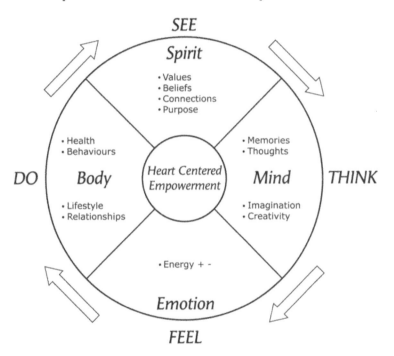

Rapid *Change*

Introduction:
Be the Best Version of You –
Mentally

Our thoughts have power – they create our world, they directly affect our relationships and health, and they are directly linked to our beliefs. So when something like a thought has so much power over our lives, it is critical to realize when it is detrimental to our life and best self.

Like many, we all suffer from the pain of our own thoughts. And like many, most of us have at one time or another thought, "I don't know what I'm doing," or "I suck at this." Thoughts like these don't do anything to better the situation; they only lead to feelings of anxiety and anger. They might not be thoughts that occupy us every day, but they can still have a negative effect on our life.

As we become more aware of our thought patterns, we grow more adept at identifying what needs to be transformed. If we feel depressed, angry, or fearful we can begin to track the cause by attentively monitoring our thoughts. Our thoughts are who we are – they are our own creations residing within us and we affect the outcome of events through our thoughts.

Understanding this, we realize just how capable our thoughts are of creating certain events, outcomes, and realities in our life. In order to create the best version of ourselves, we need to overcome and transform any thoughts that cause damage, pain, and fear.

Fay Thompson

Fay Thompson is a Licensed Spiritual Health Coach, Spiritual Teacher, Energy Master, and International Author of the acclaimed book, "Azez Medicine: Healing the Mind, Body, & Spirit with the Help of The Beings of the Light." Fay has unique insight into the subconscious mind and specializes in Subconscious Mind Correction – a technique that changes the limiting beliefs in the subconscious at the root of the cause. She also is skilled in energetic soul healing and connection. Fay is also planning a spiritual pilgrimage for those who wish to visit the sacred sites of Israel and Jordan, thus adding Spiritual Tour Guide to her long list of titles.

Fay's work has been featured on CBC Radio and TV, Voice America, and in various journals and magazines including Pure Magazine, Whole life Journal, and Well Being Magazine.

Fay resides on an acreage just outside of Saskatoon, SK, Canada with her wonderful husband and two beautiful daughters who keep her inspired, laughing, and well-grounded.

For more information on Fay and her work, visit **www.faythompson. com** or follow her on Facebook at **www.facebook.com/faythompson8**.

LESSON 9

MAKE YOUR LIFE HAPPEN!

By Fay Thompson

Ever been so busy worrying about if your life is happening the way you'd like it that you forget to live your life they way you'd like to? I've done this countless times. It truly is a lesson in futility, because the more you worry that things may not be happening the way you'd like, they aren't.

I, like most people, have difficulty living and staying in the moment, just enjoying what is happening as it is happening. To help, I began a practice of paying particularly close attention to my thoughts. I never realized how much time I spend trying to control my future. It surprised me how much energy I put towards asking questions such as: "Is it happening?" "Will everything be ok?" "What am I not doing?" "What am I doing wrong?" Aaaaaagh. These crazy thoughts may seem like I am focused on creating my perfect future, but really they are only distracting me from having an enjoyable life. Every moment I spend in anxiety, worry, trying, or doubting is a moment spent in pain – not joy.

I am primarily a future dweller – one whose thoughts are most often focused upon the future. This creates anxiety and worry. Others out there are past dwellers. They spend their energy on reliving the glory days or with the belief that the past equals the future. Both these scenarios create depression in people. They don't feel there is anything better ahead.

Whether you are a past or future dweller, the answer lies in the present. By bringing our awareness back to center, in the moment we are in, we find peace, hope, and the space to make decisions we can act upon now.

To help me assuage my anxious futuristic thoughts, I began to adopt a practice of every morning, not allowing myself to get out of bed until I could feel grateful for things in my life and excited that I am alive to experience this day. I realized I had put myself in a rut of waking and thinking, "Oh, it's morning. Nooooooooooo…" The truth is this is not how I wish to think or feel at all. I want to feel grateful and excited about my day. I believe everyone does. I found I just needed to make a decision to choose a different way of thinking the moment I woke up in the morning. This decision has changed my life. I now feel ridiculously grateful for the many blessings in my life and for the things coming my way in the future. I also found that by staying more present, I was able to make concrete plans for the future and put them into action with ease. The time I spent living in the future constantly wondering if everything was going to go my way was now being used to make decisions that led me directly to where I wanted to go. I was living instead of worrying.

As a result of this change, I have gone from having a safe, comfortable, boring life with a business that was not really growing to a life filled with adventure and prosperity. I began making decisions to be an exhibitor in trade shows which boosted my business and visibility. I began traveling, which is something I love to do, and broadened my client base. I most recently took a life changing trip to Israel (a dream come true), and am continuing to marry business with pleasure, by deciding to take groups to Israel so that they may experience the wondrous sacred sites and beautiful energy this ancient land has to offer. This may not seem like much to you, but being a spiritual tour guide is something I used to dream of. Now, instead of wondering if it could happen, it's happening. Why? Because I decided to stop worrying about my future and instead spend my energy on making my future happen.

Perhaps you can recognize part of your story in mine. Perhaps you are dwelling either in the past or future, wasting the time away from truly living. If so, and if you truly wish to decide to change this, I offer you some tips that have helped me get to where I am now. It is my deepest wish that you are able to capitalize on them as I have. They truly work.

First, let go of angst, worry, doomsday thoughts about the future, and anger that the past has not met your expectations. This requires you to smile and perhaps even laugh a little. Lightening up is the key. Get very non-serious about everything you have taken seriously. Perhaps there is something beautiful awaiting you this day. Wonder what it is. Allow yourself silly school girl notions of love, harmony, and miracles. If you are one to scoff at those who dare to dream or feel something beautiful, then you are one to deny yourself the joy of possibility.

Next, take stock of all that is good in your life. Imagine if something weren't there at all and see if you'd miss it. Your bed, your job, your mate – whatever it is, if it or they were not there anymore, and there was no replacement, would you be in mourning? If so, then you have something or someone good in your life, for better or worse. There is so much good. Everyone has sunshine, grass, flowers, trees, and nature to enjoy. The birds sing for us all. The butterflies flutter for anyone who notices. Let the good outweigh the bad. Let the abundance outweigh the lack. Why? Because it does! Experience the truth of that.

Stop telling a sob story. This may sound harsh, but it truly stops you from living a happy story. Stop talking about how people have done you wrong or how the government is corrupt or how you never catch a break. STOP. In every instance of retelling your sob story, you recreate it day by day. A change in your life story requires a change in the story you're telling. Change "I hate my job" to "This job is helping me move into something more fulfilling. I am lucky." Change "That person is annoying (or mean or rude, etc.)" to "That person is having a string of bad days. I wish them happiness so that they can feel better about themselves and others. I feel good that I am able to be kind even when others around me are not." Feel the truth of your new story and your life story will change fast.

Also, stop beating yourself up or thinking the world is crumbling around you every time something unwanted happens. Trust me, if your life is seemingly crumbling around you, it's not. It is falling into place. You can't have change without change. The old ways have to go, so let it fall apart knowing it is all coming together beautifully. Be kind to yourself while it is happening. Let yourself get mad or scared, but then allow yourself also to laugh at the insanity and believe in a brighter future. Hope is not for the weak. It is for those who dare to dream of something greater for themselves.

Finally, instead of seeing yourself or others as wrong, send love. This is compassion. The guy who honks and gives you the finger isn't really mad at you. He's mad at his life. Send him love so that he can feel at peace. Laugh that he thinks giving you the finger can make him feel better and laugh at the truth that laughing at this makes you feel better. No matter what the perceived injustice, send love. Remember to send love to yourself too. Send love to yourself when you think you've said or done something stupid. Send love to yourself when you allow yourself to feel upset at someone else's actions. Send love to yourself just because you can. Imagine receiving flowers or accolades every day at work. That's what it feels like when you receive the love you send yourself.

Dare to feel love and joy instead of judgment. Feel joy for your day instead of judging it before it happens. Feel love for your neighbor instead of judging them for their annoying behavior. Feel love for yourself instead of tearing yourself apart because you should have known better. What good does all the judging, hating, and ridicule do for you? Nothing, other than satisfy the ego's need to be right about how things should be. But if you don't feel good, it's not right. Think and feel loving thoughts. It always will be right and good.

Please know that I am not perfect and I in no way am in a loving state every moment of my day, nor should you think you must be. However, I have realized every moment I add in love is a moment not spent in hate. Every moment I allow to be in lightheartedness and kindness is a moment I feel lighthearted and kind. This is the life I have chosen to create. To choose it, I had to choose not to entertain my anxious thoughts of whether or not things were happening for me or whether or not I was enough. No one could give it to me, and my life was just not going to suddenly change unless I did.

Remember, your happy future is created by choosing happiness in the present moment. Be present with this moment. Choose to make decisions that will bring happy results. Will going on that trip make you happy? Then, in this moment, make a decision that gets you one step closer, whether that means putting away money on a weekly basis that you never touch or rearranging your schedule to take the time off or doing research about where to stay and what to do. Will having a new job bring more joy into your life? Then, in this moment decide you will get there, by enrolling in a class that will give you skills, or volunteering your time in a place to get experience, or planning your resignation. If you want it, you must be present and decide to make it happen. Only you can do that. By doing it, you stay present and you take action. You feel energized and alive. Most importantly, you spend time living instead of worrying.

Your life is yours to create. Don't let worries rob you of the time you can spend making choices in the direction of making your dreams reality. Dream big. Live big. Stay present. And, above all else, remember anything is possible.

Lotus Nguyen

Lotus Nguyen is a mindfulness coach. Through her Heart-Mindfulness™ programs, she helps entrepreneurs unleash their inner power to effectively deal with challenges. Born in Vietnam, Lotus has been an entrepreneur since a teenager when she became the family's breadwinner. Her background as a Buddhist practitioner allowed her to get through the toughest times when she worked as a filmmaker for fifteen years in the UK. Lotus has dedicated her life to finding a perfect balance of Eastern philosophy and Western lifestyle, mastering the art of applying ancient practices of mindfulness for modern-day impact. When she isn't coaching, she relishes the Argentinean tango.

www.LotusNguyen.com

📞 **+44 7947 070 598**

Ⓢ **LotusLTNguyen**

✉ **lotus@LotusNguyen.com**

⑧ **facebook.com/lotus.lt.nguyen**

in **uk.linkedin.com/in/lotusnguyen**

LESSON 10

THE POWER OF HEART-MINDFULNESS™ FINDING PEACE IN CHAOS

By Lotus Nguyen

"A trained mind brings happiness; an untrained mind brings suffering."

~ The Buddha

Our mind is like a wild horse carrying us in different directions, most of the time to our own detriment. We need to train and tame it so we can ride it in the direction that we want. Mindfulness is a magical strategy we can use to conquer this wild beast.

I am happy to say that with mindfulness training, my horse has been tamed and I am firmly on my path, enjoying the ride. These days I can have peace and joy in my daily life while dealing effectively with life's inevitable challenges.

It was not this way in my past. I grew up in Vietnam where life after the war was tough. As a young girl, I already became the breadwinner supporting my family. I came to England as a young woman after finishing university in Saigon. I worked my way up to become a film director and producer making documentaries for British and international broadcasters.

On the surface it looked like I was an accomplished, successful and competent woman. I had a good job and my late husband was a wonderful friend and soul mate. Friends looked at me with envy for the good life that I seemingly had.

Little did they know that deep down, my heart was wrenched with sorrow, loneliness and despair. I relied on external sources for my happiness and as a result I felt deeply unfulfilled. I put others' welfare over mine and did not listen to my heart. My voice was stuck in my throat as I was unable to express my true self. In the end, like a well that had been used up without replenishment, I was dried up.

Then I encountered mindfulness, and this practice transformed my life. Finally I was home, a place where I felt peace and love. I now fully accept myself, appreciate my goodness and revel in the beauty of life. I connect deeply to my body, heart and mind. I understand and love myself and, as a result, I can understand and love others well. I am more skillful in my relationships with others. I can speak the truth without fears of being judged or hurt. These days, life is rich and fulfilling. I am also stronger and more resilient to face life's ups and downs with calmness and clarity. In the midst of "ten thousand joys and ten thousands sorrows" I stay free, peaceful, and happy.

Mindfulness has scientifically been proven a powerful tool for productivity, healing and well-being. Originating from Buddhism, it has been taken on wholeheartedly by the West. It has grown exponentially in many areas of life from hospitals to schools, from sports to wellness, from individual practices to corporate management.

However I feel that while Western mindfulness-based approaches are beneficial in their own rights, they focus on the outer symptoms but do not address the underlying causes. Dealing with the roots of our deep unhappiness is the basis of Buddhism. As a Buddhist practitioner since the age of twelve, I have come to understand the Buddhist essence and use it as a strategy for my personal and professional life in the West. My aspiration is to reconnect mindfulness to its roots while making it relevant to modern daily life, easy to understand and simple to practice.

I spent two years tossing and turning at night thinking of a way to combine the scientific approach with the 2,500-year-old wisdom into one single system that any of us can understand and relate to. With my own experience and insights coming out of my practice, I have created a Heart-Mindfulness™ system first based on the two-wing approach of heart and mind, then the four-step process POVA:

Present, Observation, Value, Action™ and finally the 5 Rs meditation formula: Recognize, Release, Reflect, Relax, Refresh™.

THE TWO WINGS – HEART AND MIND

In order to free yourself from your own afflictions and fly like a bird, you need to have two wings: a wing of loving kindness and a wing of pure awareness.

Loving kindness is an altruistic and positive attitude to the well-being of yourself and others. It comes from the heart and manifests in your values and morals. Love gives life meaning and purpose as well as pleasure and happiness.

Pure awareness is a conscious state of mind that is associated with being non-judgmental, flexible and curious. Awareness leads to understanding, insight and wisdom so you can see the roots of your unhappiness. As Thich Nhat Hanh notes, wisdom is like "the sword that can cut through our sufferings."

The combination of the two wings enables you to face life's ups and downs with more equanimity, encountering less stress and confusion and experiencing more joy and inner peace.

Heart-Mindfulness™ training develops conscious awareness and focused attention and cultivates compassion and loving kindness.

THE POVA™

Based on the two-winged approach, you can follow the POVA™ process. The POVA™ enables you to become more aware of your behavior and interaction, respond skillfully to events in your life and to past patterns of behavior, and act consciously in line with your values.

P – Present: Connect with the present moment and fully engage in your experience. Use the breath as an anchor to bring your mind back to your body.

O – Observation: Observe what is going on within you and around you by paying attention to your body, feelings, thoughts and perceptions.

V – Value: Connect with your heart-based values that guide your actions.

A – Action: Take committed action which manifests in your thoughts, speech and deed.

THE 5 RS™

The final piece of Heart-Mindfulness™ involves the use of the 5 Rs™. This formula can be applied to mindfulness meditation and practice. It is particularly effective for mindful pause.

- **Recognize**: Bring awareness to your experience in each moment: your thoughts, feelings, and bodily sensations. Accept and observe both good and bad experiences, not wishing pleasant ones to last nor unpleasant ones to stop.

- **Release**: Release any holding or tension and let go of any controlling. Let it be, without trying to make anything happen nor rejecting anything.

- **Reflect**: Watch life unfolding in each moment. Be curious and look into its ever-changing, unsatisfactory and impersonal nature.

- **Relax**: Relax but stay alert. Bring kindness, softness, and gentleness to your body, heart and mind. Rest in stillness and relish in inner peace.

- **Refresh**: Refresh with a smile, gratitude and appreciation. Expand your awareness and reconnect with the world around you as you resume your activity.

Five tips to apply the Heart-Mindfulness™ system to your daily life at work and at home:

1. **Meditation**: Practice ten to twenty minutes of meditation using the 5 Rs each day. (It is much easier to practice by listening

to a guided meditation. Visit my website to download free guided meditations).

2. **The Art of Sensibility**: Develop your awareness of internal bodily sensations:

    • Pause anytime and notice five things. See, hear, smell, taste, touch for a couple of minutes.

    • Scan different parts of your body internally when you have quiet moments whether resting in a park or lying in bed.

3. **Mindful Pause**: Pause at every opportunity throughout the day: during breaks, between tasks, drinking tea, in supermarket lines, at traffic lights, etc. Use the 5Rs™ to come back to the present moment and connect with yourself and the energies around you. It is particularly helpful when you find yourself stressed, preoccupied and out of touch.

4. **Mindful Activities**: Choose to do an activity mindfully per week. Then increase more activities as you go along such as eat, drink, talk, shave, brush teeth, shower, iron, cook dinner, wash the dishes, put the garbage out, play with the kids, drive the car, do gardening, work out at the gym, listen to music, stretch, walk, run, dance, sing, make love, make a cup of tea, and so on.

    Activities such as morning routines or domestic chores that are mundane, boring or frustrating can become a joyful experience when you bring Heart-Mindfulness™ into your action.

5. **Mindful Gratitude**: Write five daily gratitudes before going to sleep. You will find your appreciation of life will bring you joy and fulfillment. With wholesome thoughts and feelings, you will feel relaxed and fall into sleep peacefully.

Heart-Mindfulness™ is easy to practice as you can integrate it into your busy life at your convenience with little effort or time. However you need to practice it consistently and long enough to make it your second nature. Habits are very strong and you can easily fall off the path. So it is advisable to join a mindfulness group for support and encouragement.

The wild horse can have a difficult temper but with kindness and wisdom, you will be able to harness its energy. Soon you will be on your way and enjoy riding on your newly tamed horse.

Cari Moffet

Cari Moffet is a veteran Registered Massage Therapist since 1998. She has owned and operated numerous massage businesses and is currently the owner of Wholelife Wellness Inc. in Meadow Lake, Saskatchewan, Canada. She is a certified Life Coach and has recently launched the Mentoring Program for Therapists to help those struggling in their massage businesses. Cari loves dreaming, creating, writing, traveling, playing piano, drinking wine and, most of all, giving and receiving massage. Cari teaches classes in meditation, dream journaling and massage coaching.

Contact Cari via:

www.carimoffet.com

www.wholelifewellness.ca

 (1) 306-236-6633

 carimoffet@hotmail.com

 facebook.com/cari.moffet

 @carin4wellness

 linkedin.com/pub/cari-moffet/37/47b/93

DREAM WRITER

By Cari Moffet

The lights were dim, the music softly playing, the speaker was taking us inward to our greatest desires in life. "Dream," she said. "If time and money were of no concern, what would you be doing with your life?" I started writing. I'd pay off my credit card, my student loan, my… "Dream bigger," she said louder, and so I responded on paper of my greatest desires, hidden out of fear of being seen. I'd have a business, go on a couple holidays per year, I would… "Dream even bigger than that," she said over the speaker system, as though from the heavens. The music got louder, I seemed to get more excited and my pen was flying off the page with anticipation… I want to create a Retreat Center where people come and experience healing in natural ways. There would be many treatment rooms, a studio, a product wall, we'd hold classes; it would be an awesome healing environment.

That was 1999. I was in my first year of business as a Massage Therapist. The clinic I worked for took all members to this seminar in Las Vegas in hopes we would develop a greater understanding of Chiropractic. Who knew this 90 minutes of Dream Journaling would change my life as I know it today?

Nineteen ninety-nine was the year I filed for divorce. My husband at the time didn't want to be married anymore. I was crushed. The ache was like none I had ever experienced. I was kidding myself to think it was supposed to work. No, life had larger plans and this divorce was part of it.

Picking up my crushed soul, I went for counseling. I was there almost a year. During that time I was instructed to journal. Write out my feelings, get them out of my body. Sometimes it would be letters.

Some would be sent and others ceremoniously burned. It was all good. It was all healing.

A few years later, having forgotten my experience in Las Vegas, I was in the market to purchase a home, but not just any home. It had to have very specific details. I wrote them all out: must be a character home by the river, have a separate entrance for my massage clientele, have separate working and living areas, and require only low maintenance because I was on my own now.

I knew exactly what I wanted. My realtor didn't waste any time. I was shown 10 properties or so and I just didn't see it. She took me back to one of the first we had looked at and started pointing out my list of wants and what it presented. She gave me a different perspective with everything this house actually had.

It took a couple of weeks until the paperwork went through, but when the call came in that the keys were going to be handed over, things started to click in for me. I am a homeowner! I have just received everything on my list! I have just been given everything I asked for. The BIG GUY was listening! The UNIVERSE loves me! I cried and cried and cried. I was in such shock and felt so extremely blessed. I knew what I wanted, I wrote it out and it appeared like magic. It seemed so simple.

Let's fast forward to 2006. My new and improved husband (who is actually a Chiropractor and was at the same seminar in 1999) and I just arrived back to my hometown in little Meadow Lake, Saskatchewan, Canada from London, England. We had lived in England for a couple of years. It was amazing to be able to travel so easily and yet the business side of leasing a Chiropractic clinic was quite difficult. We had big plans of purchasing a clinic in Alberta, Canada and were just stopping in to visit family for a few weeks as he was temporarily filling in for the local Chiropractor. As the weeks went on, we realized the business deal for this new adventure in Alberta was not going to work out and were left wondering, "What now?"

We had an offer to work in Meadow Lake at the local clinic, and so we started our life in a town I had been away from for 15 years and said I'd never return to. It didn't take long before I realized that in those 15 years away, I had gained some incredible insights into looking after my body, mind and spirit through my experiences and training. The space I rented soon became too small for all this creativity that was flooding through my mind. I started thinking of how cool it would be to have a center where I could offer all that I know and bring in people to offer what they know and help each other grow in health and wellness within the community. I wanted to create a Retreat Center where people could come and experience healing in natural ways. There would be many treatment rooms, a studio, a product wall, we'd hold classes; it would be an awesome healing environment.

Property was found and once again the keys were in my hands as I cried in private humility knowing how blessed I was and how thankful I was to be trusted with this huge task ahead of me.

How did that just happen? I was in disbelief and, yet, it felt incredibly natural. I started using more of what I had learned in Las Vegas to find a contractor, to think on the design, to find people to help me, and even to deal with difficult confronting conversations.

What do you really want in life?

A year ago we completed our second expansion into 3600 square feet. We have a staff of ten now, and can easily say we are northern Saskatchewan's largest Wellness Center.

This method of creating is not magic or "a secret;" it is available to anyone and everyone. Many have already tapped into this way of creating their lives, and you can too. A major key to it all is becoming still. How much time in your day is filled with silence, where you can connect to this Innate Intelligence for guidance, support and love?

Are you ready to create the life you desire? Here are some support steps:

Step 1: **Get Silent**. Find a beautiful journal and a pen that writes well as this will enhance your desire for writing. Set some nice music on and make a cup of tea. Sit in your favorite spot and go within.

Step 2: **Write it out.** What do you want? If you get stuck, here is a beautiful question that I use in workshops and even at interviews for our office. "If time and money were of no concern, what would I be doing with my life?" This will find your real passion. Get crystal clear. The more details you can see or write down, the easier it is to make decisions and the easier it is for God/the Universe to give you what you want.

Step 3: **Know your WHY**. As one speaker told us, "If your Why doesn't make you cry, it isn't a strong enough desire." If you don't know why you want this desire, you will most likely quit during the hard days. This is like your vision statement, possibly your purpose in life or your contribution to mankind.

Get as specific as you can and write lots. Dream, then write, and dream, then write. The clearer you can see this dream, the greater chance it has in appearing. When you are fuzzy or unsure, there is a hesitation from the Universe/God, as it does not know what you are asking for and so your desire may just linger.

Lastly, do what you can to make this desire possible. I was just at a seminar this past weekend and the instructor said, "Do what you can without stress and the 'how' is left up to the Universe to orchestrate." It is here you may learn some trust issues and how the perfect timing to your project is not always your perfect timing. In any project, there are many people involved to make it happen. I'm sure to date there have been over 200 people who have helped make Wholelife Wellness what it is today. You can think of your life as a play. The Director has to align many players. The play will happen but it will happen in its own timing. Your job is to do what you can to assist the Director.

There will be a day when you realize the play is complete. All that you dreamed, wrote out and asked for has come to you. You will take a humble bow and the lights will go dim; they will let you rest for a moment. It won't be long before you will hear that voice, "Dream. Dream bigger. Dream even bigger than that!"

If time and money were of no concern, what else would you like to do with your life?

Colleen Humphries

Colleen Humphries is an RN, Reiki Master, author, and certified Law of Attraction Life Coach for nurses and other professional women who are suffering from the burnout that affects their lives mentally, emotionally, physically, and spiritually.

She is an author of the collaborative book, "F.A.I.T.H – Finding Answers in the Heart" and the upcoming book "No Longer Creating by Default, The ABCs of Deliberately Creating Your Life."

Colleen can be heard on her radio show Think About It, an all-holistic, alternative, outside-the-box, and universal-law based program to give the listeners something to "think about" to move them forward in their lives.

Radio Show on: www.PWNradio.net

www.ColleenHumphries.com

- colleen@colleenhumphries.com
- facebook.com/colleen.kahlerhumphries
- pinterest.com/ColleenRNCoach
- twitter.com/ColleenRNCoach
- linkedin.com/pub/colleen-humphries40/a59/860

THINK FEEL MANIFEST

By Colleen Humphries

I can remember in grade school science class hearing that everything had energy, even rocks. I thought, "How can rocks have energy? They are not moving. Amazing." I would look at different knick knacks throughout the house from time to time to see if they had moved even the slightest little bit. At an early age I was fascinated with energy.

I started in nursing when I was sixteen years old and became a registered nurse in my early twenties. Even at sixteen I felt like something was missing in the medical world. That energy thing was still in the back of my mind and I knew there was something more to it, but what?

When I first heard about holistic and alternative energy healing I was in my early twenties and more than intrigued. But then . . . early in my nursing career I started to feel burned out. I did not know how to tell anyone because I felt guilt and shame for not loving what was such a noble profession. It seemed like everyone around me loved their job and I did not. I liked it some days. I even loved it on occasion. For the most part I did not. I actually started to hate it. What was wrong with me? I felt like there was something more for me to do, but I did not know what. I wanted to learn more about holistic and alternative healing, but I did not know where to turn. The internet was not around at that time.

I had some books to read, but felt too tired to read after work. I felt like if I put any more information in my brain it would explode. And yet on the inside, I was exploding. I started to have some drinks after work to relax. It began innocently enough, but over time I needed to have a drink to relax. It felt like after a few drinks I could finally breathe.

At work I was a monster. I ranted and raged. I could not handle the pressure. OMG! This was not how I wanted to be. I wanted to be . . . dat-dat-dat-dah . . . Super Nurse. Do it all and be it all for everyone. I wanted to be the person everyone could come to for help with any kind of problems.

I switched to straight night shift because I thought that would be easier on me, less people, less politics and less stress. Not! My drinking increased. I drank in the morning after work. Hey, it was my happy hour time!

My interest in energy and energy medicine took a detour as the bottle took over. The more burned out I felt, the more I needed to drink. I had to relax somehow. I changed jobs with the thought and intention that the new job would be less stressful. It was all day shift, Monday – Friday. I thought for sure I would feel better. It lasted three weeks before I had an explosion in front of a coworker. I literally became an F-Bomb dropping, trash-can kicking, chart-throwing nurse, drowning in the sea of emotions and alcohol.

Within four months of working at the new job, I got my first DWI. I was not ready to admit that I was an alcoholic. I did not want to be "one of those people."

I wanted to get a back to my energy "stuff." I still felt a passion for it. If I could just let go of that dang-blasted bottle. Over the next 5 years, I became totally unapproachable to my coworkers. I so wanted to change. I heard Dr. Wayne Dyer's audio book on "Change Your Thoughts, Change Your Life." I knew he was right. I knew it in my bones. What I did not know was that the alcohol that I was consuming controlled some of my thinking. The other part I did not know was that the other thoughts I had at any given time were also controlling my thinking.

I learned about Reiki, energy healing and in November of 2002 I became a Reiki I practitioner. In February of 2003, I received a DUI.

OMG! I stood on the side of the road defeated and I knew, "This sh%*t has to stop."

I got into a program of Recovery through Alcoholics Anonymous and my life began to change. Through the Twelve Steps, I changed. My thinking changed. My life changed.

One day I came across Louise Hay's book, "You Can Heal Your Life." She wrote about the energy of our bodies, our thoughts, our emotions and even our beliefs. It made so much sense to me. I was on my way to learn about what fascinated me oh-so-long ago.

Then . . . "It" happened! I was introduced to Abraham-Hicks and the Universal laws. Like, OMG! The information made perfectly clear sense to me.

We live in an energy-based universe. Everything is energy. Thoughts are things. And those things (thoughts) have energy (emotions = energy in motion) that is transmitted out into the universe for it to be matched back to us. I felt like I had struck gold.

While my life totally changed in becoming sober, my life was again changing in a whole other direction. I finally understood why I had burnout. I kept having the same negative, low energy-filled, life-sucking thoughts on a daily basis. So with that I created the situations to go to go along with those thoughts. The more negatively I thought and felt, the more negative situations I created for myself. The more I could not stand something, the more of the same I received. The more I hated something, the more I got it in my face . . . over and over. My burned-out mind reproduced more burned-out thoughts. They multiplied feverishly.

When I got sober the burnout I felt decreased, but I had a long way to go. When I learned about the Universal laws and how important my thoughts and emotions really were (and are) in how I attract to me and how I manifest, I knew I was on my way to changing my whole life.

It is not about God or anybody else doing something to me. It's all about me and what I am thinking, feeling and vibrating all of the time. I can control my thoughts once I recognize that I am thinking a negative thought or feeling out of alignment with happiness and joy, or bliss as Abraham-Hicks puts it.

What I started to do was set my intention for my day to be good, fun-filled, and helpful to others. I chose to have fun and be happy when other people around me were not. I chose to focus on what I wanted and I allowed others to be how they were.

No, I was not perfect at it by any means. I gave up perfection and Super Nurse wanna-be ideation so I could be more in the flow and ease of life.

A year prior to my introduction to the Universal laws, life coaching came into my life. I thought that was an interesting concept, but nothing was tickling my fancy. After a couple of years of learning more about the Universal laws and deliberate creation, I came across a Law of Attraction Life Coaching program. That was it. That was the program for me.

I became a certified Law of Attraction life coach and chose to work with nurses and other professional women in burnout. It made sense to me. My burnout almost cost me my job on more than one occasion. My burnout started in my head and was pouring out of me by way of my emotions. Only I could change it by changing my thoughts, my beliefs, my feelings and emotions.

I would choose a better feeling thought most of the time when I noticed that I was not feeling so happy, or if something in my life was not going the way I wanted it to go. I took a step back and saw how I created my situation. I still use my Louise Hay book. I look at me, where I am, where I want to be, and where I want to go. I focus on "what do I want?" "Why do I want it?" It's OK to want things. It's how the Universe expands. And a very important aspect upon which I focus is "How do I want to feel in the having of what I want?" "Oooo lala!"

One of the biggest ways to manifesting is getting into the feeling of what you want. If you have a difficult time doing that, think about whatever makes you feel good, and go from there. My cat Petals is my "good-feeling-go-to." Once I feel good, because of my thoughts about how sweet and precious she is, I then think about what I want to manifest... and I'm off!

Lauren Heistad

Lauren Heistad is an Intuitive Spiritual Healer, inspirational speaker, psychic medium, and author of the book "Activating your SOULworks – A Healing Journey." Lauren provides individual and group healing services, teaches others about energy healing, and proactively inspires others to understand and believe in our God-given abilities to make a positive impact in our world. Lauren is the founder of SOULworks Sacred Healing Centre in Saskatoon, SK, Canada. This modern-day spiritual facility provides a tranquil space for people to experience and expand their connection with spirit.

For more information on Lauren and her work, visit:

www.soulworks.pro

SOULworks Sacred Healing Centre: 3-2228 Avenue C North, Saskatoon, Saskatchewan Canada

📞 **306-652-5555**

✉ **Lauren@soulworks.pro**

f **facebook.com/SOULworks.Intuitive.Healing**

f **facebook.com/SOULworksSacredHealingCentre**

f **facebook.com/activatingyourSOULworks**

DEVELOPING A MIRACLE MENTALITY

By Lauren Heistad

"Miracles come in moments. Be ready and willing."

~ Wayne Dyer

As an Intuitive Healer, I have been blessed my entire life with many miracles and wondrous demonstrations of the Divine. The first life-changing miracle occurred over twenty years ago when I was brought out of a deep slumber by an angel. The angel delivered a clear message to send healing energy to my Mom along with a vivid vision of her going into cardiac arrest. What moves this story from one of panic to one of miraculous wonder was the moment I followed my heart and utilized my God-given abilities to send healing energies and loving intentions towards my Mom. It was within that exact moment of following my guidance and believing in the Divine, both above and within myself, that a miracle began to unfold.

Since that harmonious moment with Spirit, I have spent much of my life learning to understand how my visions and actions helped facilitate a miracle. More importantly, I have pondered and learned how to move from experiencing one random miracle to the point of co-creating these wondrous moments of glory day after day.

What I have come to understand is that although faith in the Divine is certainly a significant factor in the creation of miracles, the main component to a magically inspired life involves moving out of the logical mind and into the heart. When we learn to trust our feelings and propel ourselves forward during moments of inspiration we are living with a "Miracle Mentality." We are setting ourselves up to receive astounding and uplifting moments through intricate synchronicities and breathtaking connections with the Divine.

On the night of my Mom's cardiac arrest over 100 kilometers away, my logical mind could have moved into skepticism and doubt: Was the angelic visitation even real, why would my healthy young Mom be sick, and who was I to think I could help? Instead, while submerged in the actual event, I chose to follow my heart and my intuition; a decision I am forever thankful for. I often wonder what would have transpired if I had simply rolled over and gone back to sleep. How would our lives have been different if I had dismissed my shocking but accurate visions? Don't get me wrong – the actual event and determination to survive a cardiac arrest was and always will be my Mom's own decision at a soul level. However, my involvement in this miraculous moment changed both of our lives forever. For myself, this event initiated my intuitive healing abilities, it opened my eyes to the unknown, and it single-handedly started my lifelong pursuit to evolve my connection to spirit. In truth, this moment completely activated my SOULworks. If I had simply gone back to sleep without a second thought of the inspirations and visions I was receiving, the astounding changes to my own life would never have played out the way they have.

Now the interesting discovery I have made along the way is that miracles happen all the time. However, whether we decide to integrate them into our own lives is a totally different story. You see, to activate these miraculous moments, we actually have to honor our feelings and choose to engage in those gentle nudges from the Soul. We must then move forward with our own free will during moments of inspiration in order to magically intertwine these miracles into each and every day.

Imagine if the next miracle in your life was scheduled for 2:00 yesterday when you were inspired and truly felt like connecting with a friend. This connection at the right time and the right place could have led to a ripple effect of numerous big and small life-fulfilling changes. However, instead of following that inspiration, you let your logical mind get in the way by saying things like, "I don't have time for a visit right now," or "I should really spend my day doing something more constructive like cleaning the house."

Now don't get me wrong, that is not to say the universe won't create more and more synchronistic events to help bring your dreams into reality, nor does it mean you never need to clean your house again! What it means is that if you were to let your life unfold by following your feelings and inspirations, your days would become much more meaningful and miraculous.

We humans tend to think we are the most advanced species on the planet and yet we are the only ones no longer utilizing our intuition on a daily basis. Can you imagine a world where animals use their logical minds instead of their instincts to make their decisions? If this were the case, animals would avoid gut feelings such as the instinctual urge to seek higher ground before a life threatening storm; but instead to stay home to clean the den! Silly yes, but my point is clear. Over time, we have stopped utilizing our intuitive instincts on a day-to-day basis and have instead become completely focused on the logical mind.

Now I am not saying we should eliminate our logical mind and cognitive mental processes. What I am saying is our intuition and how we actually FEEL should be our first priority. Once we assess our feelings, we can then use our logical minds to help propel these moments of inspiration forward.

Inspiration is our Spirit speaking to us from a Soul level. When we ignore inspiration, we are ignoring our true heart's desires and the glorious possibilities our conscious minds have not even fathomed yet. Miracles unfold when we take the time to listen to and follow the navigational path of our Soul. Learn to completely trust and follow these insights. As you move further and further into trusting the divine order of all things, your manifestations will become quicker, grander in scale, and more miraculous every day.

I am forever humbled by the experience of divine intervention with my Mom. What I am truly grateful and proud of is the simple fact that I followed my heart. Even though the entire experience was new and unknown, I did not let my logical mind tell me I was making the vision up. I did not let my ego tell me I was stupid to think I could make a difference. I did not refuse to take action because it was easier to simply roll over and go back to sleep. Instead, I followed my heart and jumped in with all my instincts intact.

To quote a dear spirit guide of mine, "You have to keep ignoring the logical mind and instead follow the illogical heart until you get to the point that it only makes logical sense to follow your heart." That is how to develop a "Miracle Mentality."

Here are a few practical tips to help you create your own Rapid Change into a Miracle Mentality:

1. Honor how you feel. Read a book when you are inspired to read. Clean your house when you are inspired to clean (if you wait long enough, the inspiration will come!). Make changes in your life when you are inspired to change.

2. If you are trying to make a big life decision, take the time to feel each scenario within your heart. Even when your logical mind does not think you have an opinion, if given the opportunity to speak, your heart will always show you how it truly feels.

3. Follow your inspirations. If you get the idea to stop by a new store in town, stop. If you are inspired to take a new class or workshop, register. If you overhear an idea that provides inspiration, follow it. Give yourself permission to live intuitively.

4. Utilize at least one day a week to move through the entire day only when and how you are truly inspired. If this means staying in bed until you are inspired to get up, do it. If this means heading out of town on a last minute travel opportunity simply because you were inspired, go for it.

5. Give thanks for all the miracles and synchronicities in your life, big or small. These moments are helping define your life and unfolding new opportunities of magic along your journey.

6. Avoid following old patterns. When you notice you do the very same thing day in and day out, shake it up a little and inspire yourself to create a change. It is when you are not

living on autopilot that you are more apt to notice the nudges and guidance along the way.

7. Expect miracles always while believing in the magnificent power within you and the Divine to create change.

8. Strive to make your heart a priority, your mind connected to all that is, and your faith centered on the Divine. In doing so, you will begin to develop your "Miracle Mentality;" a state of being that is truly more logical and magical then first meets the eye.

Sheridan Genrich

Sheridan Genrich is fiercely committed to empowering overworked businesswomen to find clarity of mind, natural weight loss and renewed energy, so they can focus on their goals in life. After spending 15 years as flight attendant she intimately understands how to improve her client's health no matter how hectic their schedule.

Sheridan earned her Bachelor of Health Science degree in Complimentary Medicine from Charles Sturt University. She also holds Advanced Diplomas in Naturopathy, Nutritional Medicine and Herbal Medicine. She is a Certified Health and Wellness Coach and is currently completing her Masters in Neuroscience at the University of Queensland.

www.refreshhealthnow.com

www.falundafa.org

✉ **sheridan@refreshnow.com.au**

❶ **facebook.com/refreshnow.wellness**

🔗 **linkedin.com/in/sheridangenrich**

LESSON 14

UNLEASH THE POWER OF YOUR MIND TO CREATE ENDLESS PRODUCTIVITY WITH EASE

By Sheridan Genrich

Artists are all too familiar with their greatest works manifesting after times of turmoil. Somewhere in the midst of challenges and massive change we tap into creativity or a clearer path. The harder our external world becomes, the more we are forced to manage our internal world, just to survive.

While I'm not an artist, I'm a sensitive soul who's faced those times. As I look back on the most significant times, they actually offered me opportunities to find the courage to listen for the connection between my heart and mind. Ultimately, I would find the best course.

My journey on the road to find my best health was clear from an early age. Like other sensitive souls I would feel things. Meaning, I would feel more sensitive in my body, chemistry, emotion and digestion than the average person, so there was a need to be continuously aware. Negative people, foods, strong perfumes, chemicals, irritating music, loud sounds or poor air quality could all affect my well-being. For sensitive souls it's common to often react very quickly when something around them doesn't serve them in mind and body. One turning point for me was the year of my twenty-seventh birthday when I faced close relationship changes.

Major break-ups are stressful, life-changing events. They take us into uncharted territory. The strain can leave us feeling physically paralyzed and emotionally vulnerable. Everything is disrupted: routine and responsibilities, home life, finances, relationships with extended family and friends, and even your identity. That year was the end of a six-year-long marriage. To make matters worse, around the same time my parents were going through their own divorce after 27 years of marriage.

At the time I was a flight attendant with an erratic shift-work schedule involving a lot of travel. Friends were transient and hard to keep in close contact or catch up with, as I was always on the move. I was standing on a pillar alone, with all the foundations around me crumbling.

I felt disappointed and uncertain about my future. My inability to cope, feeling miserable and depressed for months on end, forced me to start looking for solutions. I sought healing through acupuncture, yoga, herbal medicine from my naturopath, changing my diet and exercising madly. These things all gave me some temporary relief, but in a way, I was running away from looking inside myself to find peace in my heart. Sorting through a myriad of conflicting opinions on health made me frustrated and unsure if I'd ever find what was true for myself.

While on holidays in San Francisco I had the good fortune to be handed some information about a free Chinese meditation practice. It so happened that the same meditation classes were also held not far from my home. I thought I had nothing to lose, so I starting attending the weekly classes. Unlike other meditation or yoga I'd done in the past this one was to beautiful instrumental music and was instantly relaxing. I didn't need to focus on my breathing and could follow along to the five simple exercises. I was feeling peaceful and content for the first time in years and was hooked. The volunteer instructor emphasized to me that Falun Dafa was a practice of mind and body, so its greatest benefits came doing the exercises while applying its principles of Truthfulness, Compassion and Tolerance to daily life and reading a book that went with it. Little by little, with these amazing tools, I began clearing the rubbish away from my mind. With the constant chatter and worries silenced, I became a lot more positive and gained strength.

I was fascinated to learn that the traditional Chinese character for medicine comprised the two symbols of music and herbs. Pondering further on this one evening, not long after I moved to a new home, I had an "aha" moment. "I no longer want to be passive. I know nature has the answers if we want to listen. I must study natural medicine so I can not only heal myself but help others too."

Within a few weeks, I was enrolled into what would eventually become eight years of study in nutrition, naturopathy and herbal medicine, all while I was still traveling for work nearly every week. Each time I learned something that theoretically resonated with me I'd try it out and see how it felt.

When the challenges of jet lag hit hard, when I lacked natural air and light, and when I craved fresh unprocessed food, I relied on a few key areas to pull me through, so I could mentally focus in order to be productive enough to write assignments or study for exams. These basics form the foundation of good mental health with physical benefits too:

- **Create Your Own Routines & Rituals**
- **Lifestyle Eating, Never Dieting**
- **Using Tools of Traditional Medicine**

CREATE YOUR OWN ROUTINES & RITUALS

- When your work or lifestyle dictates a crazy shift-work schedule, you must get creative with your routine in order to stay in control. Routines organize us, providing structure and meaning to our lives. By grounding yourself with regular wellness practices you'll bounce back faster. Employ mini-rituals for tranquil exercises like meditation or even reading a book to wind down. Screen media aren't ideal as they switch off melatonin, the sleep hormone.

- Ask for support before you desperately need it.

- Then there are a few really obvious rituals to follow often, no matter where you are in the world. While they may seem basic they're often overlooked:

- Listen to your body's sleep requirements. Each person needs a different amount but the general 7-8 hour rule applies to most. Sleep clears out mental clutter and unimportant thoughts. Getting a good night's sleep can also be the difference between a sharp memory and feeling forgetful.

- Only eat until ¾ full – don't overeat. Try adopting the habits of the Okinawan Japanese and eat only until you're no longer hungry. It takes around 20 minutes for your brain to register that you're full.

- Reduce excessive alcohol consumption. Alcohol in moderation isn't terrible for the brain but too much alcohol is damaging to brain health and function. Alcohol can cause memory problems and encourage foggy, disorganized thinking.

- Eat breakfast. It kick starts your metabolism and unlike coffee on its own, it can stabilize your blood sugar (depending on what you choose to eat, of course).

LIFESTYLE EATING, NEVER DIETING

Too many people comment about being on a "diet" when they start eating healthier, rather than just taking control of their eating habits and saying, "This is just the way I eat!" The fewer processed foods you eat, the more efficient your digestion. Digestion directly affects your brain function via the enteric nervous system. Actually 90% of your serotonin (the mood neurotransmitter) is found in your gut. If you're going through massive change, then the more efficiently your body is functioning the better you'll adapt. You'll be able to not only survive but thrive!

For boosting brain power there are some specific proven foods to do the job. These include walnuts, green leafy veggies – smoothies are great for this – and going wheat-free is a must if gluten-free is too much of a stretch. Wheat in particular causes brain fog for many people. Plus don't forget fiber to stabilize blood sugar and suppress your appetite, also necessary for a clear mind.

USING TOOLS OF TRADITIONAL MEDICINE

Meditate regularly. Meditation has been known to relieve stress, increase IQ and promotes higher levels of brain functioning. Meditation also activates the prefrontal cortex of the brain, an area responsible for advanced thinking ability and performance. There's also evidence that it strengthens your immune system too.

Listen to classical or instrumental music. In order to truly relax and learn, it's important to listen to rhythms of 50-70 beats per minute, as they're similar to pulses of the human heartbeat at rest. This type of music activates the left hemisphere of the brain, which is why it often helps students do better in mathematics and writing. Actually, there's been an 80% increase in spatial intelligence scores seen in those listening to Mozart.

Take scientifically researched herbal medicines. Bacopa monnieri and Gingko biloba have scientifically been shown to significantly increase blood flow to the brain. Increased blood flow to the brain is correlated with an increase in focus and problem solving.

Now don't get overwhelmed and think I don't have days where I'm not totally fried. But I do implement many of these things at least 80% of the time. There's nothing like a productivity workout to build my enthusiasm and stamina. And when loads of projects have to get done, this is how I thrive. So take a look at your own business and life. How can you proactively use some examples from these three areas to be more efficient and positive about the work you need to do?

Maia Stewart

Maia Stewart is an author, healer, business entrepreneur and busy mom who founded The Lotus Room Healing Centre in Labrador, Gold Coast, Australia. She has made it her life's work to help others break out of the box and live the life of their dreams.

Maia has been interviewed around the world, written articles and home study courses, and has spoken publicly about her work.

Her thriving business, The Lotus Room, offers relief of stress, anxiety, fatigue and generational baggage and promotes peace, prosperity, fulfillment and success in all areas of life.

Contact Maia:

www.thelotusroom.org

(+61 Aus.) 0410 973 410

maia.stewart2

thelotusroom01@gmail.com

facebook.com/thelotusroom01healing

Maia A Stewart @thelotusroom01

LESSON 15

FREE YOUR MIND AND LOVE YOURSELF

By Maia Stewart

I was a busy mum (mum or mom?) with three children who became tired and run down. Trying to run a business and look after the house was exhausting – at one point I could hardly lift my arms. Since then I have been on a healing journey and have learned to change my negative thought patterns that directly affect my world, heal generational baggage and limiting beliefs and have learned to love and heal myself. This has helped me to transform into a relaxed, loving mother and successful entrepreneur.

Being able to love yourself, break free of society's mold and create a life that you love is such a liberating feeling. We are all taught from a young age that we need to work hard in a job we often don't love and to strive for certain things that we don't actually desire, but this can come at the cost of our happiness. A balance of material comfort and peace of mind is so uplifting. Many of our thoughts are not even created by us, they are conceptions based on the views we think others have. We can choose our own thoughts every minute of the day, we can decide whether to entertain a thought or not, before it can take hold.

If we have been mistreated in our lives we are quick to do this to ourselves and others, but if we realize this and see the reality that others are living in we can create all that we need and keep it. We can be taught when we are young not to love ourselves, not to be "selfish," but sometimes the only way we can help others is to make sure we are happy and healthy first. Generational baggage, limiting beliefs and pain can also be passed down, causing all sorts of anxieties and self-doubt in our lives. These can govern our every move without us even knowing about it. Teachers, schools and the media also create other stereotypes and unrealistic demands. We can be forced to shut down when our minds are overloaded with critical self-judgment and extravagant expectations from those around us. It is okay, if we have reached the point of total exhaustion, to care for ourselves. If we don't take charge of our own lives, our health and total life force can begin to diminish. Let's try to Love ourselves before this happens; we can be "super mum (mom?)" and look after ourselves as well.

Self-love, understanding and forgiveness is the key to success. Acknowledgement and realization that we are just human and everybody makes mistakes is how we learn. Now it is time for us to love ourselves; it is natural and the simplest way to create a life of bliss for everyone. When we get to a crossroads in our life we are shown how to love and care for ourselves, to wake up and see clearly what is happening.

There is a principal in Taoism that says we all travel along in our day-to-day lives until we are awakened. It could be by a car accident, job loss, or illness, anything of big significance that shocks us and makes us assess our lives. We realize that we haven't been taking care of ourselves or seeing the bigger picture. Once this crisis happens we are open to healing and changing everything. We can feel like, "No, I don't want this," "this isn't right," or "there has to be something more!" We can change our lives anyway, but it is hard to get moving if you are comfortable where you are.

Finding the courage and stepping away from what seems normal can be difficult, but if you are certain that you want rapid change in your life it will happen. You can become conscious of your thoughts and free yourself with your mind. As you begin to heal and see how the Universe works, you can start to change your priorities as well. When you see that all you have has been created by you and that your thoughts have created this, you become so humbled. Then you can learn and see all the power you actually have. Everything is energy and everything is pliable. You can make a difference.

Our thoughts have been found to be measurable energetic frequencies, which means they directly affect our surroundings as well as our obvious decisions. You create your own Universe with your mind; everything in existence has been created with thought, and if we elevate our thoughts and emotions we attract new and better experiences. If everything vibrates at different speeds, we just need to change our vibration. This means being happier, healthier or just believing you are or will be soon. True peace comes when our life is ready, not when we think, "I will be peaceful when my life is perfect." If like attracts like then we need to be what we want in order to attract it – "fake it 'til you make it." Happiness, health, respect and abundance – all of these will come to us when we are giving and being these things. When we begin to realize these methods, we have begun to open the door to our ultimate and complete happiness.

Healing the spiritual heart is another important part of our success. Removing limiting beliefs, childhood baggage and heartache is how we move forward with the most passion and purpose. Our hearts become damaged and covered over, they close off and we follow our erratic heads instead. If we peel back the protective layers that have formed we can access our full potential. Coming back to the heart and asking for it to be healed is the quickest way to see all that could be.

Once we forgive ourselves and others for all their wrongdoings we are open to all the Love in the Universe. By accepting our mistakes and seeing others as just different learning beings we open and heal our hearts. Our heart is meant to lead us; when we forgive and heal, we allow our heart the input it is meant to have. We can listen to its caring reflection and gain new insight to all the possibilities for us. By connecting to the Universe and the Creator of everything through our heart, we can access all abundance, see all peace and know everything we need to do.

Meditation is one of the fastest ways to connect to our true heart. Meditation does not only help our bodies physiologically, but it helps calm our minds and our hearts as well. Meditation can be the starting point for your life of progress. A simple guide follows:

- Sit quietly with your eyes shut and focus on your breathing.
- Breathe deeply and see yourself surrounded with soft, Loving light.

- See a beam of light coming down from above, gently entering your head and moving down to your heart space.

- Feel the Love all around you, let go of all fears, the Love will protect you.

- Remember your thoughts and feelings that have been causing you trouble.

- Ask the Love how they can be healed, then listen, relax and trust.

- Notice any thoughts or feelings that come into your mind.

- Let these answers open your heart and see all solutions.

- Stay here and breathe, feel Loved and feel protected.

- Know you have begun and know that you have gentle strength and Love within you.

- Come back when you are ready, open your eyes and feel peace.

- Write down your new insight on how to proceed.

- Know you can come back here at any time and connect with the Universe. Feel peace in knowing you are connected, you are one and you are always supported if only you allow it.

It can be as simple as this, listening to your heart, honoring yourself and your true feelings. Find your goals again, feel like you can achieve them, know you can have anything you need. All of our goals, even from childhood, are definitely possible, and all of our peace is already within us. Sitting quietly reminds us of our strength, power and peace and can bring the consciousness of our spiritual self. We all contain this accessible peace inside and with practice we can find it. To be able free our minds and love ourselves is such a gratifying gift. Grasping the fact that we choose how we think, we choose how we act, and we choose all we have can bring perfect well-being.

It has been proven that at the end of the day, it is up to us to create the life we want. You too can free yourself of worry and anxiety. You can open and free your mind and lovingly heal your heart. You can break away the layers and reveal your true self, find your power and peace within and build the life of your dreams. The answer is in your heart and your heart knows best; it will reveal everything to you when you are ready.

Rapid Results Whole Self Wheel

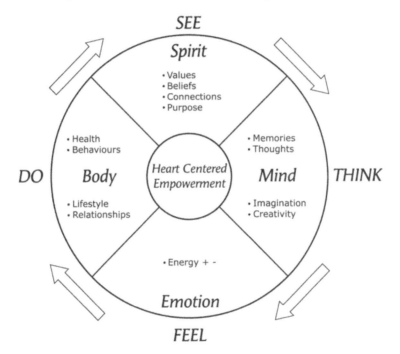

Introduction:
Be the Best Version of You
Emotionally

Emotions can range from feelings of love, tenderness, and compassion, to anger, frustration, and sadness, and they can last for just a moment or persist for days, weeks, or even months. How we learn to control our emotions is through two awareness processes: first, we must identify the thought that immediately preceded the emotions, and second we must identify shifts in the physical state through body sensations and feedback from others.

To expand on this, we must understand that the word "emotion" better describes a person's energy state, while the word "feeling" points to our perception of an emotion through cues from our body. What we believe affects what we think, and what we think immediately creates our emotional state, which in turn immediately affects our physical state.

Regardless of what emotions we feel, it is important to become more aware of how we feel our emotions and why we experience them. Being in touch with our feelings is a rich source of information and experience. Plus, it helps us better connect to our intuition. And when our emotions are of high frequency energy (feelings of love, acceptance, respect, joy, and appreciation) instead of negative, heavy energy, we are capable of being our best self.

Roxana Boglio Branigan,
MA, NCC

Roxana Branigan is a board certified clinical counselor, certified coach, entrepreneur, author, mother and wife. Roxana's academic achievements include a master's in clinical mental health counseling, coaching certifications and an international business degree. She is also the creator of the ROCK IT Revolution™ and her ROCK IT System™ a proven 6-step formula that empowers women to take complete control of their life, health, success, and ultimately their happiness. Time is precious! Don't waste another hour of it heading in the wrong direction or being bashed by the waves. Even if you've hit rock bottom, Roxana can help you break through the self-limiting beliefs that are holding you back. A new life awaits. Are YOU ready to ROCK IT?

If you are ready to live your life to the fullest, and you are interested in finding out how Roxana's ROCK IT Revolution™ can help, contact her:

www.roxanabranigan.com

✉ **rbranigan@me.com**

f **facebook.com/RoxanaBranigan**

twitter.com/RoxanaBranigan

in **linkedin.com/pub/roxana-branigan-cpc-crc/0/a4/827**

TRANSITION WITH CONVICTION: OWN YOUR BREAKUP AND ROCK IT!

By Roxana Boglio Branigan, MA, NCC

Every year, thousands of couples end their marriage in divorce, leaving in its wake a whirlwind of emotions. There is confusion, fear, loneliness, desperation, and underlying all of it, a profound and unshakable sense of loss. It doesn't matter how bad the marriage was or how "over" things we are; something dies inside of us.

As a woman, these feelings are compounded by a million hard questions... How will I survive financially? What's going to happen to the kids? What will my friends think? Will I ever find love again? I asked myself these same questions and as difficult as divorce was, it also showed me how strong I am.

In life, we can either make choices ourselves or let our lives be dictated by the choices of others. We can choose to move forward, even if we take the smallest of steps, or live forever in regret of what could have been. I'm going to show you several practical steps to help you ROCK your divorce. Not only do you have the power to survive a breakup, but you can walk away a stronger and better person because of it.

I married a man I thought I would spend the rest of my life with. I was raised Catholic where divorce is looked down upon. I had never experienced it growing up (my parents openly loved each other), and it wasn't something that got talked about, either.

I had not been married long before I began to feel that something was seriously wrong with our relationship.

Then one day, I woke up. It was like an out of body experience. I looked down on my life, but only saw a shadow of who I was. I saw myself walking, talking, and doing, but I was dead inside. Where had I gone? I had lost my essence, my spark, my ability to ROCK life. In a flash of awareness, I suddenly realized that I no longer even spoke to my very close friends. I had been under my husband's control for so long that I didn't even realize what was happening to me.

We shared a home and a child, but it felt more like a prison. The one thing that kept me from leaving sooner was our son. I did not want him to grow up in a broken home. But I came to the realization that it would be better to give my son a healthy environment, even if it was not perfect, rather than stay married and constantly expose him to all the negative energy and experiences.

My professional life was successful, but my marriage was a disaster and a nanny was raising my child. Here I was – a Catholic – with a child and getting a divorce. This was one transition I never thought I would ever have to go through. The guilt was excruciating, but life with my ex was worse. I summoned all my strength and made the choice to reclaim myself so I could provide a healthy, stable life for my son.

I had reached the tipping point. Something needed to change and fast! So, I did. I made changes professionally and personally. For the first time in years, I felt I could breathe again! My life was getting back on track. I truly felt I OWNED my life again, and I would fully ROCK IT!

Now that you have heard about my transformation, let me share with you 8 strategies on how I did it, so that you too can take back your life, OWN it, and ROCK IT!

1. THERE IS A DIFFERENCE BETWEEN BREAKUP AND BREAKDOWN

The truth is that there is a huge difference between breaking up and breaking down. Use the past to empower you and learn from it, viewing the experience as a learning curve you had to go through in order to find your true inner strength.

In order to become our true selves we first have to get to know who we are, and then have the confidence to show that personality to the world. Once we do, we can begin to grow and expand our consciousness and reach out for the love we truly deserve.

To help you OWN your breakup, here are 5 things to remember:

1. Accept that it is over.
2. Focus on the positive.
3. Keep reminding yourself this is what you want.
4. Use positive affirmations.
5. Remember life is short.

2. EMPOWERMENT LIES WITHIN, NOT WITHOUT

If you want to OWN your life and ROCK IT, you have to discover your internal strength. A breakup can leave you feeling powerless and weak, but it does not have to. You can cultivate empowerment from your soul and nourish it so that it guides your life and sets the new standards for what you will accept and what you will not.

If you want to learn how to empower yourself, apply these 5 simple, yet powerful, steps:

1. Find a role model and emulate her behavior.
2. View your breakup as a learning experience to grow from.
3. Have big dreams and aspirations.
4. Do not give up, EVER!
5. Own your life and ROCK IT!

3. OVERCOMING FEAR

Fear is our greatest enemy. It causes us to make irrational decisions that are often based on illogical thinking. The fear that divorced women experience is directly related to the fear of change. How will I pay all the bills? What will people think of me? Can I really be happy without him? Will I have friends left? By overcoming these thoughts and answering them with positive responses women everywhere can challenge themselves to OWN their new lives and grow towards a better way of living. Overcoming the negative aspects of fear will give you the greatest gift ever – FREEDOM.

4. CHOOSING TO HEAL

Healing from your relationship can be one of the hardest parts of the breakup. It comes through acceptance, and when you choose to accept the situation you are in, only then can you truly ROCK IT and OWN IT. Envisioning all the things that create excitement in your soul ignites the healing process.

Here are 6 steps on how you can get yourself to choose healing:

1. Accept that your life will never be the same.
2. Envision a positive outcome for your new life.
3. Gather your dreams and aspirations.
4. Write down your goals, and design a five-year plan for your life.
5. Take stock of your talents, and create a new resume.
6. Choose the future life you want, and OWN your decision.

5. FOCUS YOUR ENERGY ON THE RIGHT THINGS

Wherever you choose to focus your thoughts and energy, that is where you will be. Going through a breakup can deflate you and take your focus off the things that matter the most.

If you want to change your focus, you need to shift your thinking. To see this principle in action, try thinking about only positive things for one full day. Instead of saying, "I know I'm going to be late for work," say, "I am confident I will arrive just in time." You will clearly see that the way you think impacts the outcome of your life!

You can learn to refocus your energy in 3 ways:

1. Channel negative thoughts into positive ones.

2. Develop a healthy exercise and diet routine. You'd be surprised the impact food has on our mood, so try to eat healthy whole foods.

3. Engage in new hobbies that distract your mind while enlightening it.

6. LEARNING HOW TO EVOLVE

The word "evolution" signifies the gradual development of a simple identity into something more complex. As women, we go through many changes in our lives. We can either accept this change and embrace it, or we can spend the rest of our lives fighting it. I finally evolved to the point where I can now say I am ROCKing my life and loving every minute of it.

Here are the 4 vital things you need to do in order to evolve into the woman you want to be:

1. Genuinely look at your life and eliminate the obstacles holding you back.

2. Believe in yourself.

3. Look at your breakup as a clean slate you can evolve from.

4. Surround yourself with positive people.

7. TRUSTING YOURSELF

It can be difficult right after a breakup to believe that you have made the right decision. But if you want to ROCK your new life you have to trust yourself.

Learn to trust your mind by understanding that it is your stronghold. As women, we have the power to bring our emotional strength together with our intellectual strength, and that is a very powerful combination!

8. OWNING YOUR DECISION AND LIVING IT UP!

Own your decision, trust your mind and believe you are capable of handling anything that life sends your way. The future awaits you with blessings and memories that you cannot even imagine.

3 Ways to Live it UP!

1. Praise your decision.
2. Use your breakup to accomplish new things.
3. Spend time with your girlfriends.

I have seen it a thousand times in the women who embrace change and work with it instead of fighting it. You can have that same freedom! Choose life instead of pain and rejection.

9. WHERE DO YOU GO FROM HERE?

Through my personal experience with women all over the world, I have learned that most of us do not realize how truly amazing we are. That is the reason I have developed a business that helps women go through every challenge they face with grace and dignity. If you make the effort to follow the advice above, you will find that your breakup will be the smoothest transition you've ever faced in your life. Take life by the horns and make it work to your advantage by **OWNING** your life and **ROCKING IT!**

Jen Bugajsky, AADP

Jen Bugajsky is a health and body relationship coach, an expert at empowering women to invest the time and energy to improve the health of their family. Jen's education and experience improving the health of her own family have equipped her with extensive knowledge in holistic nutrition, health coaching and teaching women how to love their bodies. She works with clients to help them in making the dietary and lifestyle mindset changes that produce lasting results. Clients love Jen's ability to take the fear and stress out of where to begin by focusing on one simple step at a time.

For additional tips and strategies on transforming the health of your family:

Naperville, Illinois

www.onepowerfulstep.com

📞 **331-444-2281**

✉ **Jen@onepowerfulstep.com**

f **facebook.com/onepowerfulstep?fref=ts**

𝓟 **pinterest.com/jenbugajsky**

in **linkedin.com/in/onepowerfulstep**

YOUR BODY IS YOUR GUIDE TO RECLAIMING YOUR TRUTH

By Jen Bugajsky, AADP

"If you listen to your body whisper then you don't have to hear it scream."

~ Author Unknown

I believe that God created us to live full, vibrant lives and gave us the power to heal our bodies naturally. We all have the answers we need within ourselves, but there are so many lies, misconceptions, stories and confusing messages in today's world that many struggle to find the truth. To me, finding your truth begins with listening to your body.

I will admit I didn't always know what it meant to listen to my body. It's a skill most of us must develop. In my quest, I prayed and thought I was doing all of the "right" things, but I still felt trapped. I soon learned, put simply, that most of us "think" instead of "feel." Our ability to tap into inner wisdom is within us, but we have forgotten or have never learned to use it.

Although I was brought up in the Catholic faith, I was never taught how to listen to the wisdom of my body. It wasn't until recently that I learned to tap into my emotions and let my body be my guide. When I allowed myself to feel and trust, doors began to open, and when this happens, we can learn to reclaim our truth by letting go of our ego and our plans. We can be still and allow ourselves to feel. Our inner guide allows us, with ease and grace, to fully embrace our truth and become the best version of ourselves.

Two key tools that helped me with this are the Art of Feminine Presence (AFP) and the Emotional Freedom Technique (or EFT, also referred to as "tapping"). AFP showed me how to be grounded and centered within my own energy. When fully present, I can use my body as a guide. There is a natural shift from within that aligns me with my authentic self and allows change to flow with grace and ease to live my life purpose. EFT allowed me to use my body to get in touch with my emotions. EFT uses elements of Cognitive and Exposure Therapy, and combines them with Acupressure, in the form of fingertip tapping on 12 acupuncture points. With EFT, I found I was able to dig deeper within myself and unseat the excuses of why I couldn't do things. They were really masks for something else. I just had to figure out what.

Eventually, I relied upon these strategies as life challenged me to reclaim my truth through my children, my career and my marriage.

Five years ago, two of my boys were diagnosed with serious health conditions including ADHD, learning disability, speech and development delay along with sensory processing disorder. When I prayed for help, God revealed that I needed to reclaim my own truth. Problem was, I didn't know how to do that.

Everyone told me to put my children on medications, however I didn't listen to outside forces. I felt in my gut there was another way. I then buried myself into learning everything I could about health and nutrition to help my family. My decision to heal my children naturally has guided my journey to places I never thought I'd go.

For example, I became a certified health coach. I had been walking blindly in faith, but I now trust my inner guidance. There have been many obstacles in my way as I considered whether or not I was doing the "right" things. I would constantly feel the little devil on one side saying, "Is this truly the right thing?" and the little angel on the other side saying, "Trust and believe, and this will guide you to the truth." However, I grounded myself, dug deep, used EFT and my listening skills, and was able to discern what felt right.

Another powerful example of this was illustrated in my marriage. The story begins with me praying to improve my marriage. I asked for this multiple times, but continued to feel stumped. I thought I had the tools I needed, but there was something in the way.

On my 40th birthday, my husband and I attended a Marriage Encounter small group discussion. That day, my body showed me what I needed to know. As we sat in the circle, I could feel my heart racing, my palms sweating and my body shaking. My heart wanted me to share with the group, even though I was scared to death. When I finally did, I cried in joy, embarrassment, emptiness and sadness. No one judged me. They loved me for being raw, open, and vulnerable. I was in my own truth.

I decided I would put faith at the center of my marriage. Even though I had tried before, I wasn't aware of the real truth holding me back. The following day I had a vivid dream. I don't normally have dreams, so this was surreal. The dream was that my husband was with another beautiful, sexy, feminine woman.

At first I couldn't understand what my body was telling me. I had prayed for help in my marriage and now my body shows me this! This woman was so different from me!

Most of my life I have played more of a masculine role. I work full time, am the breadwinner of my family and have four boys. I never thought of myself as "girly," but why did I attract so much masculine energy? What stories did I create in my head? What purpose were they fulfilling? Why did I shy away from being feminine?

I needed to dig deeper and find out what my body was telling me. I later realized the woman in the dream was me. But why did I look like someone else? Why was I hiding? Oh my! I didn't believe that I was beautiful, sexy and feminine. Why didn't I believe in myself?

As I continued to dig deeper, new information was revealed. There were times I fought myself saying things like, "Could this be for real?" But each day, I sought the truth. When I allowed myself to be vulnerable and tapped into what was awakening for me, my body revealed the truth using all of my senses. I experienced dreams, back pain, chills down my spine, laryngitis, tears, visual images, whispers, messages through music, opportune passages from the Bible and so much more. When I learned how to be centered and tune into my heart, my emotions and suppressed memories, I received the truth to let go and be free.

I learned in a few months what many fail to unravel or sadly never understand after years of therapy. I am not broken. There is no race to win. I am beautiful, confident, smart, feminine, sexy and amazing. I love and respect myself, and my body is a temple that is guiding my path.

Tapping into the wisdom of your body and reclaiming your truth is powerful, yet challenging. Here are some practical tips on how create rapid change:

- **Pray for Your Self (Focused Intention)** We are used to praying for the sick or the needs of others, but also spend time asking for what you need.

- **Spiritual Practice (Be Centered)** Believe in a higher power, be still and relax. Get grounded and listen. (i.e., Meditation or reading the Word)

- **Awaken your Senses (Awareness)** Be open and aware of what you can see/imagine, feel/touch, hear (words or sound), taste, smell (breathe). Use your body and your senses as a guide.

- **Body Confessions (Feel)** Tap and feel into it. Once your body tells you the truth, acknowledge and embrace the feelings; don't deny them.

- **Power of the Body (Stay Open)** We only use 5% of our consciousness; the other 95% is subconscious. Be courageous and trust your body. Don't be afraid to listen to what you might find. The truth will set you free.

- **Forgive and Let Go (Release)** Allow your body to feel the emotions. Express/feel the pain, release and let it go (forgive yourself and/or others).

- **My Soul My Voice (Rejoice)** Give yourself permission to worship and praise the spirit within. Honor, appreciate and love yourself.

Now I am on a mission to share my story and help women and young girls learn to love and respect themselves fully, focus on proper nutrition for their family, and tap into their own body's wisdom. The best gift a mother can give her child is living in her God-given feminine essence and reclaiming her truth. Learning to love yourself is also the first step in rekindling your marriage.

I challenge you to take One Powerful Step in your journey to reclaiming your truth. Learn how to be present with your intentions, ground yourself, tap into your senses and enable your body to reveal what your subconscious mind already knows.

> "The first step toward getting somewhere is deciding that you are not going to stay where you are."
>
> ~ Author Unknown

Franni Welter

Franni Welter has owned an independent health food store since 2002 and has reached many of her goals since starting her healing journey. Her desire to become a Certified Focused Intention Technique Practitioner became reality in 2011. Franni is continually creating and achieving new goals as the wisdom of her body shares messages from her heart center consciousness to do so. Franni's passion is to help people release negative emotional triggers from the core level and educate them to instill unconditional self-love. Discover your inner passion and purpose to become the greatest version of yourself. Your treasure is awaiting within.

www.naturespureenergy.com

📞 **780-340-6708**

Ⓢ **fran.welter**

✉ **naturespureenergy@gmail.com**

✉ **franwelter@shaw.ca**

🅕 **facebook.com/naturespureabundance**

g+ **plus.google.com/+FranWelter**

LESSON 18

RELEASE YOUR INNER BUTTERFLY WITH LOVE AND GRATITUDE TO SET YOURSELF FREE

By Franni Welter

It is never too late to start your healing journey or create a new dream. There is no such thing as waiting for the right time to begin your healing journey or make a positive change in your life. Magical things can happen at any time.

Life after forty has provided more learning opportunities for me than all my previous years put together. My deep desire to become an energy healer became clear when I chose to heal myself from within and live life from heart center consciousness in gratitude, joy and love. Allow the wisdom within your heart to lead you to your dreams and a new way of life now.

> "And the day came when the risk to remain tight in a bud was more painful than the risk it took to blossom."
>
> ~ Anaïs Nin

My healing journey began in 2006, when I found myself repeatedly experiencing the same negative thoughts and emotions such as anger, resentment, insecurity, anxiety and fear. With my first marriage ending in divorce, I knew that something had to change to ensure a positive outcome with my second husband.

Working at removing limited beliefs, and practicing love, gratitude, forgiveness and thankfulness, I learned to live in heart center consciousness in harmony with my body, mind and soul. Digging deep within my core to release negative emotions and limited beliefs set me free. It was astounding how my cells, heart and soul became wide open when my negative issues and triggers were eliminated, therefore allowing pure joy and happiness to fill my entire being. As I focus with intention from heart center continuing my daily practice of love and gratitude, my days are spent living my life wholeheartedly.

Paying full attention to my thoughts, blocking negative thoughts, instilling positive thoughts, exercising self love, practicing gratitude and forgiveness on a daily basis are the contributing factors to experiencing an amazing shift during the most trying time of my life.

Most of us have experienced feelings of hatred that rises up when someone has treated us wrong. Even after losing everything and having to start over, no feelings of hatred or vengeance towards the person who caused the major storm in our life entered my soul. What was truly amazing was that I felt compelled to send him thoughts of love, forgiveness and compassion. The love for myself, removing limited beliefs and gratitude for my life is the reason I can overcome trials and tribulations with grace and ease.

One day near the end of my storm, I had an epiphany: Greatness can be achieved with less. Less stress and more peace are the gifts you give yourself when you appreciate what you have at any moment and resist the need for more things.

The opportunity to become certified as a Focused Intention Technique coach became available to me in the midst of our struggles, and my immediate reaction was that it was not the right time to do it, even though I had been waiting for this opportunity for quite some time. As doubt cast its shadow over my readiness for this task, I acknowledged a message from within that my own thoughts were the only thing stopping me from achieving my dream and realized the timing was actually perfect. The training not only helped me through my storm, but fulfilling my dream to become a Certified Focused Intention Technique coach provided a positive focus. Never allow yourself to think it is not the right time to make a change. Your thoughts and choices are the only thing standing between you and your dreams.

"A positive thought that is kept for 17 seconds can raise your positive vibration equivalent to 2,000 action hours. Staying present in the moment with one positive thought for 68 seconds will expand your positive energy to 2,000,000 action hours creating a miracle."

~ Esther Hicks, "The Power of 68 Seconds"

Make every second in your day count, by ensuring you are stopping all negative thoughts, replacing them with positive ones while feeling thankfulness for everything you have in your life. Create a "gratitude now" list by writing down absolutely everything you are grateful for. Also create a "gratitude intention" list with everything you want to come into your life. Feel gratitude and imagine that it's already there. Your heart will fill with joy, happiness and love each time you think of your gratitude lists and can change your mood instantaneously. There are no limitations to achieving anything we set our mind and heart center intention into. It is incredible to see the abundance come into your lives when you start living each day this way. Simple things each day will make a huge difference.

"Powerfully intend to attract something small. Starting with something small, like a cup of coffee or a perfect parking space, is an easy way to experience the law of attraction in action. As you experience the power you have to attract, you will move on to creating much bigger things."

~ The Secret

I was on my way to a tradeshow and running late. I caught myself thinking about being late but immediately changed my thoughts to thankfulness for arriving on time. I took not one, but two wrong turns and had to laugh at myself. Remarkably, I was not late. A perfect example of how our minds can change an outcome without stress.

Daily affirmations and learning to love yourself are key to setting yourself free from inner turmoil. Louise Hay's Mirror Talk exercise is extremely valuable and should become a part of your daily regime. Push through the initial uncomfortable feeling, as you learn to love yourself. Acknowledge and honor your feelings, push through the negative emotions and tell yourself every day, "I Love you (name), I really, really love you." Before you know it, the awkwardness will be gone and your heart will fill with love when you think of or look at yourself. You will love every inch of your being, which will affect every person around you in a beautifully positive way.

"Most of the shadows of your life are caused by you standing in your own sunshine. The only thing standing between you and your dreams is your belief it is possible and your willingness to go after it."

Ralph Waldo Emerson

To accomplish living life in pure joy and happiness, make the following part of your daily ritual:

- Learn to love yourself wholeheartedly using the mirror talk method.

- Keep your awareness in the moment, stop negative thoughts and set intention to positive thoughts.

- Use affirmations to set your day in the right direction.

- Feel gratitude and thankfulness each morning, throughout the day and before you fall asleep for all the amazing things in your life.

- Add to your gratitude lists on paper and/or in your mind.

- Forgive yourself and others, keeping in mind you forgive others for your own well-being, not because they deserve it, but because your soul deserves it. You will know when you have completely forgiven someone when the hurt is gone when you think of them.

Loving yourself wholeheartedly and living with daily gratitude is the most amazing gift to self that you can offer. Self love and gratitude can set you free from inner turmoil, and the effects of negativity that may surround you in your daily life will simply feel easier to dissolve and not take personally. Realize that when people act in a negative way it is a reflection of their own inner turmoil. By instilling gratitude and love in your everyday life you will be compelled to send thoughts of love, compassion and healing to the person portraying the negative behavior.

Our bodies are remarkable and have the ability to heal. Research shows our heart has a brain of its own with 5,000 more positive energies than our primitive brain. Our hearts and cells hold our intuition and truths for our well-being and greatness. Listen to the answers from heart center and resist allowing your mind to analyze them. When you guide it, your thoughts from heart center will set you on the most incredible path to your dream life.

Being true to yourself is easy when you love and admire yourself and live in gratitude. When people undermine your desires, and dreams, predict your doom or criticize you; remember they are telling their story, not yours. Stay true to yourself because you are amazing!

I was truly blessed to find the healing modality and teachings that brought my body, heart and soul to their unlimited, incredible potential. My wish for you is that you seek out the same. Start living your life with love, gratitude and forgiveness to reawaken your remarkable, unlimited self. Release the butterfly within your soul and fly to your greatest life with grace and ease. You will thank yourself for the rest of your life.

Carmel Morgan

Carmel Morgan is the author of "Bad Girl Wisdom," to be released Fall 2014. She lives in beautiful Petaluma CA with her honey and her fur babies. Carmel's professional passion is teaching, coaching and training wounded women how to create their own heart chakra makeovers for themselves and how to heal the emotional body with chakra yoga therapy. Carmel fell in love with Somatic Healing and Quantum Healing at IPSB in Culver City, and it changed her life forever. Carmel is a Pioneer of Chakra Yoga Therapy for Healing Heartbreak and Bad Girl Wisdom Leadership Breakthrough Trainings.

www.carmelmorgan.com/rapid-change.html

✉ **badgirlwisdom@gmail.com**

f **facebook.com/pages/Bad-Girl-Wisdom/193503530854118**

▶ **youtube.com/channel/UCftpWBBQHaocMCkaZ2EzWfQ**

LESSON 19

SOME BAD GIRL WISDOM ON HOW TO TRANSFORM HEARTBREAK INTO HEART-POWER WITH A HEART CHAKRA MAKE-OVER

By Carmel Morgan

MY LIFE GAME PLAN

I am a fellow traveler on the river of life. I am here to pay forward my story to Wounded Women, Warriors, Healers, Teachers and Artists. The details of who did what to break my heart no longer matter to me. My focus is on creating more heartpower, being a river guide to those who want to learn how to do their own heart chakra makeovers, and teaching women how to be leaders with their heartpower. Are you ready to let go of your heartbreak and step into your heartpower? I used to hit my head on my own glass ceiling over and over. One day after I sincerely sang my "why not me" blues, one more time, my yoga teacher quietly stated that the best day of her life was when she broke up with the word SHOULD. She said, "The key to a woman's success is to do more of what you love & less of what you SHOULD." It baked my noodle. For so long the quest was to look for what and who can fix what was broken inside me.

Seriously. I had done my time in self-help aisles, therapy rooms, 12-step meetings and yoga retreats. Peeling the onion was becoming exhausting and I burned out on my quest to transform my bad girl past into a good girl success model of working hard and self-sacrifice. You know what I mean if you have spent hours in a pity party, ugly, coping and wrestling feelings fat with pain. Of course there is no magic pill to suddenly give us all self worth and wipe away years of inner turmoil. What I did learn is that my magic reveals in a simple daily practice that is focused on embracing the kaleidoscope of experience of being a woman.

A woman's heart can be her greatest treasure or her greatest weapon. When we focus our mojo, we can transform our body and our life. My Chakra Yoga Therapy Practice that healed my traumas, dramas and karmas is the result of years of professional and personal study in the fields of Holistic Health, Quantum Learning Sciences, Yoga and Bodywork. I worked on one issue at a time and I learned to value myself and this how I do it.

MY BIG WHY

I am one of every three women in the U.S who has survived sexual trauma and violence. On Valentine's Day, I dance with One Billion Rising to celebrate our lives. I have invited other women, but they were busy or do not want to dance in public. One time, my invitation brought an awkward silence, worse than if I had dared let a fart slip. Of course one of us will step up as a good girl, check to see if I am ok and change the subject. I once got, "Would you like gluten free or regular crust?" Yeah. THIS WAS THE DAY. I got the Post-It from the Universe. We need to embrace our stories to heal our hearts. You are doing the work. Pay forward your story. Invite women to dance with you.

HEART CHAKRA MAKEOVER

What is a heart chakra? A heart chakra is the energetic field of vibrations that is given off from our heart organ. Our heart's electromagnetic field is 60 times larger than our brain's and has the same vibration as mother earth. We are able to sense danger or safety with our kinesthetic sense.

Our kinesthetic sense is also known as our women's intuition. It is what our heart's vibrations pick up from our surroundings and gives us gals octane fuel with our bountiful hormones. Fearful thoughts and heartbreak stories tear down our immune system. Love thoughts boost our immune system via the hormones that our emotions secrete.

Our emotions are carried via a web of connective tissue called fascia that joins together as bands holding a concentration of energy around the body's endocrine glands. Yoga calls these energy stations chakras. Our nervous system tells our immune system via our cells in our body how to react to everything we say or feel. We hold back emotional expression for our own safety by contracting our muscles. We keep our issues in our tissues until we are ready to heal our stories.

THE HEART CHAKRA MAKEOVER

Every woman needs to claim a space every day to manage, clean, save and grow her emotional energy, so she knows where to spend her valuable life currency.

The Heart Chakra Makeover is a practice that creates a space for us to heal the stories stuck in our emotional body. It takes 21 days to form a new habit and 90 days to make the habit a body memory. Our body's ability to heal is greater than we imagine, and when we combine our creativity and feelings with music, we lay down new neuropathways for new habits that empower us. Start your day with a 15 minute practice, filling your teacup first, so you can serve from the saucer throughout your day.

1st Key: Lighten Up

- Begin your practice with 3 deep breaths.
- Breathe out the heartbreaks that no longer serve you and breathe in gratitude for your heartpowers.

2nd Key: Follow Your GPS

- Develop your intuition muscle with small declarations of support every day that make you laugh!
- We have 70,000 thoughts a day, and when we embrace our mojo, we change our chemistry.

3rd Key: Fly Your Freak Flag

- Buy a special art journal and lots of color markers and pencils to build your right brain muscles.

- Every morning after your gratitude breaths, doodle your oohs and boos in your heart.

4th Key: Embrace Your Turtle Shell

- Create a heart chakra playlist for your phone, computer and car. Every morning, hit SHUFFLE.
- Trust the right music will play for you and dance!
- Release the Boos and invite in more of the Oooohs!
- All humans are 96% the same. Our special sauce is the 4% of our DNA that is our one of a kind, never again to repeated, our true self-expression. So love your turtle shell! This is your treasure.
- Imagine what would happen if women embraced their mojo?
- Dance alone and let the tiger out!
- Rock it!

5th Key: Surf the Feelings

- I have learned from my coaches and teachers that transformation always brings a test.
- Let yourself lean into the edges of the feelings.
- Scar tissue is the strongest foundation for building a ladder of success out of a pit of poo. Leaving our comfort zone is scary, so start with small field trips where you are most curious.
- Surf the waves...

Bonus Tip: Celebrate Yourself. All of it!

- We all have faults and mistakes that happen sometimes.
- Is it worth stealing Your Joy?
- When you catch the negative going long... just ask... is this worth stealing my joy?
- Is this worth creating stress hormones that steal my life force?
- Is it worth spending my precious breaths here?
- Do you want to choose love or fear?

- Remember it is always about celebrating your best efforts.
- Keep on Shining, You Crazy Diamonds!
- Mwah!

María Tomás-Keegan

A certified Life and Career Transitions Coach, an author and an entrepreneur, María's passion for helping women make their transitions an empowering experience comes from her own struggles through career change and life upheavals. Through María's journey to manage life's inevitable changes, she's discovered a powerful, process that has led her to breakthroughs achieving a level of peace, happiness and satisfaction beyond any expectations. For additional tips and strategies for Transcending Transitions, visit María's website and request her eBook, which shares 15 ways to ease your transition journey.

More about María here:

www.YourSafeHarborCoaching.com

Maria@YourSafeHarborCoaching.com

facebook.com/safeharborcoaching1

linkedin.com/in/mariatomaskeegan

THE SEASONS OF LIFE – DISCOVER THE MAGIC

By María Tomas-Keegan

I believe that everyone goes through life's inevitable transitions following a flow – a progression – like the seasons of nature. I have not always understood this. As I look back at the transitions in my own life, I notice the progression is the same each time.

The type of life change doesn't seem to matter. For me there have been several career transitions, two divorces, the loss of loved ones – too many to mention – a massive life-style change, relocation across country and an early retirement decision. For each one the same progression repeated.

I read something about life transitions that resonated with me in Carol McClelland's book, "The Seasons of Change." She compares the stages of transition to the seasons. Autumn, Early Winter, Winter Solstice, Late Winter, Spring and Summer. This metaphor helps me think about my personal journey through transitions. Perhaps this story will resonate with you as you consider your own experience.

Each season has a purpose in the transition process. Although it was tempting to avoid the pain and deep soul searching, it became clear to me that I could not jump from Autumn to Summer without going through Winter and Spring first. Transition is a delicate journey – one which requires awareness, support, patience and the desire to move forward, one small step at a time.

AUTUMN

"Autumn, it feels like autumn
Although the breeze is still, I feel the chill of autumn
Oh, yes, it's autumn, it's always autumn
However green the hill, to me it still is autumn."[1]

After my second divorce, it was definitely Autumn. This is a time when a transition begins. Something may catch you by surprise, perhaps a layoff, forced retirement or an unexpected pregnancy. For me, I knew something was coming – that divorce decision just had to be made – and I dreaded its ultimate arrival. In Autumn, you may experience the loss of something and feel the need to grieve. This is the time to accept that there is a change afoot. It's the first step in any transition.

It may take a bit of time to get through the Autumn season, as it did for me. Mourning the loss of my second marriage was hard to accept – I didn't want to be known as that woman who was divorced twice. "What's wrong with her?" is what I imagined people were saying. So, it took time and real soul searching to come to terms with my new, unwelcome situation.

EARLY WINTER

"They say that things just cannot grow
Beneath the winter snow
Or, so I've been told."[2]

This next season wasn't much better. I was fatigued – mentally, emotionally and physically. Things started to change all at once. I was confused and overwhelmed. Decisions were hard – very hard. I questioned so much: "Have I done the right thing?" "Should I move out of town?" "What about our mutual friends – will they divorce me, too?"

It was time to dig deep and find patience. I surrounded myself with people who supported me and brought positive energy. They encouraged me to take time and think carefully before making major decisions. They advised me to stick to a routine – get up and go to bed at the same time, go to work every day, walk the dogs often – it helped me feel safer, more normal. It took a while for things to settle; I spent a couple of months in Early Winter. It was time well spent. I learned to listen to my gut.

WINTER SOLSTICE

I finally found some hope. Although I thought this might be the darkest time, I began to feel some peace with my decision to divorce. As I reflected on my situation, my intuition told me I had made the right move.

Finding a quiet place for reflection and soul searching was helpful during this Winter Solstice – sometimes it was a physical location, other times it was a quiet state of mind.

I started to see some glimmers of light that, on the other end of this journey, I would be okay. Memories of other transitions in my life, in which I survived and thrived, brought me comfort and confidence.

LATE WINTER

Things began to change. I started to envision what my future might hold. Perhaps a major move was in order – I had no idea where yet, but it was clear to me that I wanted to leave the New York/Connecticut area for parts unknown. I was becoming inspired by the vision. I put feelers out just to see what might come to me. I took stock of where I had visited in the past to see if anywhere spoke to me – it didn't. So, I knew it had to be a new place I'd never been to before.

SPRING

"A little bird, he told me so
Open your eyes, the sky is full of butterflies …
Spring is here at last …"[3]

One evening I went to dinner at a trendy pub and piano bar with several friends. As we were chatting, this very tall and handsome man came to our table to ask if one of us would sing with him. Each and every one of my friends pointed to me. A bit nervous, I let him lead me to the piano where we sang "Unforgettable," the duet by Nat and Natalie Cole – a sign of things to come.

I had no intention of getting involved with anyone again – at least not for a long while. The Spring of my journey hit with a flourish. It happened so fast – one evening we met and sang at a piano bar, I gave him my business card, he called and we dated every weekend for months – we went to dinner and dancing (he literally swept me off my feet!), and we talked 'til the wee hours of the morning. One day, quite unexpectedly, he asked if I would join him on a trip to Arizona, where his friend was getting married. I had never been to Arizona – listening to my instincts, I said "yes."

There was an immediate spiritual connection for me in Arizona, especially in Sedona. The mountains surrounding Phoenix spoke to me, too. After 15 days of touring the area, I knew I had found my next home.

Spring brought me great energy, purpose and excitement. On the flip side, I felt restless and struggled with priorities – what to do first, second, third. I was more confident in my choices – I knew that I was on the right path. My intuition was speaking very clearly and I was listening!

SUMMER

"And the summer wind came blowin' in from across the sea
It lingered there to touch your hair and walk with me
All summer long we sang a song and then we strolled that golden sand
Two sweethearts and the summer wind."[4]

Summer finally arrived. My vision was crystal clear and I knew what steps to take to make it happen. Everything – every person that came in my path and every choice I made – fell into place as though it was meant to be. This was such an empowering time. I was on top of the world again. For me, it was finding the place I wanted to live and the man who spoke to my soul. Once we decided that being together and moving to Arizona was right for both of us, he and I each found new career opportunities in Phoenix, we sold my condo in two weeks, packed up our lives in Connecticut, put the two cats in the car and drove 2,700 miles to our new home. And, another transition began – a career change, a cultural shift, a new home, new friends AND a new marriage! Who would have thought?

This time, it was a transition of my choosing. Big difference! But, a transition nonetheless, which requires awareness, a strong network of supporters and patience until all the pieces fall into place like they are meant to be.

These transition experiences, along with my professional skills in mentoring, coaching and training, have prepared me to help other women face life's inevitable changes with more clarity, grace and peace. When we follow the pattern of the changing seasons, it serves as a guide – a GPS for the soul. Change can be faster and smoother, with more direction and an empowering outcome.

For every major life change, there is a flow, a progression. My best advice is that you honor the seasons of the change, listen and discover the direction that feels right to you. Trust that you'll know it in your heart and gut when it comes along.

When you acknowledge that a major life transition is happening, you have taken the first step. When you allow yourself the time to grieve what is lost and embrace what is coming, you will make your journey much easier and smoother. And when you get excited about the new possibilities and step out of your comfort zone to explore them – **MAGIC HAPPENS**.

References:

[1] Excerpt from "Autumn," lyrics by R. Maltby, Jr. and D. Shire

[2] Excerpt from "Winter Song," lyrics by S. Bareilles, I. Michaelson

[3] Excerpt from "Spring Fever," lyrics by G. B. Kaye

[4] Excerpt from "The Summer Wind": Lyrics by J. Mercer/H.Mayer/H. Bradtke

Linda Cimpric

On her life journey, Linda has been evolving towards open-hearted living. She is a Reiki master, Access Consciousness Bars® practitioner, and Certified Angel Card Reader. Linda passionately helps her students and clients release struggle and embrace ease. She believes Reiki is a healing tool for everyone, and can be a pharmaceutical substitute. We all have our own knowing, and Linda guides others to trust their intuition. She believes in the ability to learn to open your heart, and supports her clients to embrace this special gift.

Linda lives in Saskatoon Saskatchewan Canada, and supports clients in person, and via phone and Skype.

www.evolve-one.ca

✉ **lindacimpric@sasktel.net**

f **facebook.com/pages/Evolve-One/596708457037991**

in **ca.linkedin.com/pub/linda-cimpric/7b/bbb/895**

LESSON 21

EVOLVING TOWARDS OPEN-HEARTED LIVING

By Linda Cimpric

Both of my parents passed from this world without ever telling me, "I love you." Needless to say, in matters of the heart, I was extremely uneducated. I adopted their guarded stance, often keeping my heart closed, thinking I would be shielding myself from emotional pain. Learning to open my heart has been like attending university, and I've had many wonderful teachers.

HEART OPENING 101

I was filled with awe the day my daughter was born. The beautiful tiny baby that grew inside me was a miracle. Being helpless, I believed she was like putty in my hands, and I needed to shape her – teach her. What a foolish idea. It was she who first taught me about opening my heart. Just by interacting with her, I felt a love I'd never experienced before: patient, unconditional, endless, and my heart opened.

HEART OPENING 201

I thought I'd reached the maximum capacity for that kind of love. Although I wanted another child I was confused about where more love would come from. Then my son was born, and I felt the same sense of awe. I loved him immensely, and I didn't love my daughter any less. I was overwhelmed with joy! He taught me that my capacity to love could grow, and my heart opened further.

HEART OPENING 301

Babies are easy to love, but my children were not done with their teaching.

When my son was three he once stood in the porch for thirty minutes screaming – protesting my refusal to take off his rubber boots for him. My heart had slammed shut in anger.

When my daughter was fifteen she drove away in my van in a brief moment of independence. She did not have a driver`s license, and I did not see the humor in her actions. Again my heart had slammed shut with anger.

There were many interactions with my children where my heart had closed in fear, worry, anger, and/or frustration. Looking back, it was as if the toddler and the teenager were saying, "If I do this … will you still love me?" In the intensity of the moment it was not easy, but then after calming down I could feel the open-hearted love that was the foundation of our relationship. They taught me to say, "Yes, I will always love you."

HEART OPENING MASTER`S DEGREE

Life unfolded, I was divorced, and my present husband and his teenage daughters came into my life. His daughters played a game of whoever said "shotgun" first was entitled to the passenger seat. My husband's youngest won the honor one day, but her triumph was short-lived. They were on their way to pick me up and my husband informed her she'd be heading to the back with her sisters, and I'd be riding in the front. This did not go over well and came to symbolize our relationship. Everyone was vying for their place. Being "in the back seat" was not a welcome thing, and I was resented for it.

It took time for me to see things from the girls' perspective, which I needed to do to understand their feelings towards me. I wanted to love them – like I did my own kids, but I was lost as to how. I'd dropped into hostile territory (the teenage years) with no foundation to stand on.

During this time, my conscious "spiritual journey" started. I was searching for a different way to be in the world that would allow more ease, more peace, and more joy. I started to read. My beliefs were challenged and my thinking changed. I began to understand: we can adopt negative beliefs in childhood; our feelings reflect our own beliefs, and the actions of others reflect their beliefs and feelings. I began to see my stepdaughters as two parts – an interior, which was their Spirit, and an exterior, which were their beliefs, feelings, and actions. I realized that I didn't have to always like the exterior, but I could connect with and love the interior. This took many years and is still a work in progress. Through my relationship with my stepdaughters, I learned of a love that can start with conscious choice, and move into an open heart.

HEART OPENING
(STUMBLING UP THE STAIRS TO THE UNIVERSITY PHD PROGRAM)

My spiritual journey was evolving and I had discovered Reiki. I wanted to share this loving energy with whomever would welcome it, so I began to give treatments to friends and family, and eventually became a professional practitioner.

The more I practiced, the more I opened up to experiencing love. It shocked me the first few times I felt open-hearted love for someone whom I'd just met while giving them a treatment. The joy and gratitude I felt was very intense. I learned at a class how to use a pendulum to check whether the seven main chakras were open or closed. While holding the pendulum over the chakra, motion meant open and stillness meant closed. I began using this in my practice.

A dear friend also took the class and we arranged to meet at her house to share this knowledge with others. That morning she argued with her husband and treated him coldly. While checking her chakras, the pendulum told us that her heart chakra was closed. The rest of us moved energy, which opened her chakra. When her husband came home that evening, she opened her arms and said, "Hello honey!" He did a double-take and asked what had happened to her.

THAT WAS MY AHA MOMENT! **The physical symptom of the heart chakra being closed restricts the flow of energy of love – both giving and receiving**

Imagine a miser living on plentiful land, fed by a large river. The miser hears new neighbors will be moving in, and he's never had good experiences with others. He decides to dam the river to discourage the people. However, the dam also cuts off water to his land. He thinks he can manage by collecting rainwater. He believes this will sustain him, which it does, barely, but it causes anxiety as he always worries about when it will rain.

A person can survive without an open heart, but damming it causes struggle. We do not feel the same emotionally or physically as we do when our hearts are open. With a closed heart our quality of life is restricted. Emotionally we can feel sad, afraid, angry, vengeful etc., and physically our energy level is low and we feel "heavy." We have dis-ease.

I started studying this phenomenon on myself. Words from a loved one that "felt" painful to me would trigger a closing, but with conscious effort I realized that I could remain open. The unconscious became a part of my conscious thought. When my heart is open I feel more ease, peace, and joy.

Open-hearted interactions, regardless of the context, are easier. Interactions that once left me tense and angry now leave me feeling peaceful. The joy I feel spills into all areas of life, and I feel more connected to my true self, to other people, and to nature.

I excitedly took this knowledge into my treatment room and developed a way to teach my clients to open their hearts. Everyone realized it was simple to do, and found a benefit in the way they felt, "like a weight had been lifted."

Am I a doctor of open-hearted life? No. I've discovered the path that works for me. Although I sometimes fall off into the brambles of life, I remind myself what if feels like to be open-hearted and return to that path. It's an evolution.

Here are some steps to living open-hearted:

1. **Open your heart.** Set your intention towards opening your heart. Imagine the thick heavy curtains of a stage covering your heart area. Exhale fully. While inhaling, imagine opening the curtains fully. Envision your heart space glowing brilliantly. Feel gratitude.

2. **Practice opening your heart.** Do this preferably at the same time each day, until you can feel when you are open or closed. Awareness is the key!

3. **Let go of the past.** If a story from your past surfaces and causes discomfort, open your heart.

4. **"Difficult" person exercise.** Visualize a "difficult" person in your life and hold them in your mind's eye. Practice keeping your heart open as you say to them (in your head) something you've always hidden from them.

5. **Spirit focus.** Begin to imagine the "difficult" people in your life with an interior and exterior, and focus on the interior – their Spirit. Consciously leave your heart open during communication with them.

6. **Forgiveness.** Open your heart and forgive yourself when you struggle, and others too.

When we close our hearts, we do so because we are protecting ourselves – an act of fear. To live open-heartedly means to allow the energy of love to flow through you with complete faith in Spirit. For rapid change in how you feel, both emotionally and physically, be conscious of your heart. Be open to faith, open to energy, and open to LOVE!

Jacqueline Sonnenberg

Lifestyle coach Jacqueline Sonnenberg is a certified FIT (Focused Intention Technique) coach and offers transformational sessions with clients. She offers Holistic Retreats in Bali and teaches detox, meditation and the FIT Technique to the world. She is the owner of **Amazing Bali** website.

For more details on how to trust your intuition, please contact Jacqueline via the links below:

Seminyak, Bali

www.amazing-bali.com

+62 (0)81 339 654 230 GMT +8h

Amazing-Bali

Jacqueline@amazing-Bali.com

sunnymountain@gmail.com

facebook.com/pages/Amazing-Bali/175077016094

LESSON 22

TRUST YOUR INTUITION

By Jacqueline Sonnenberg

"The intuitive mind is a sacred gift, and the rational mind is a faithful servant. We have created a society that honors the servant and has forgotten the gift."

~ Albert Einstein

As soon as I learned to trust my intuition, my life began to change, and I found myself embarking on an incredible journey. Today I live in the beautiful, exotic Island of Bali with the love of my life. I am enjoying a newfound freedom and am happily working towards retirement.

Living the life of my dreams was always my goal, but I often got sidetracked along the way. Eventually I found a way to achieve my dreams, and today I teach others how to realize their goals and succeed in every aspect of their life.

Growing up in Switzerland, a country that is known for its banks, watches and chocolate, was great, but my childhood was rife with challenges. At the age of four I had to contend with my parents' divorce. Having to live with a mentally unfit mom who could barely support us, forced me to mature at an early age. I yearned to leave these dismal conditions and live an independent life.

After I completed my apprenticeship in a local bank, I discovered that I had a great desire to travel and explore the world. I craved freedom and adventure. I dreamed of spending my life in an exotic, tropical country, sitting under a palm tree with my laptop, and writing a literary masterpiece.

Instead, I ended up moving to Germany and getting married. I felt unfulfilled because I wasn't able to realize my dream of living abroad. A few years later my family invited me to move into their home in Portugal. "Stay with us and write your book," they said. I was elated!

My whole life changed after I accepted their offer. A few years later I divorced my husband and met Bill, who became the love of my life. We shared the same dream, traveled the world and visited many countries. After spending a few months in Bali, we fell in love with it and have lived here ever since.

Throughout most of my life I've struggled to make enough money to survive. After Bill and I met, he was the breadwinner and I was still unable to earn money and contribute. Determined to make it happen, I created a Bali-oriented website. I devoted most of my time and energy to this project with the intent of soliciting real estate clients. It proved to be a difficult undertaking. I wanted to have fun and live a life of leisure in paradise. I couldn't understand. Why it was so difficult for me to attain financial success, while so many others seemed to achieve their goals effortlessly?

In 2011 I met Loretta Mohl, the well-known creator of the FIT (Focused Intention Technique) Mindset System. She taught me how to reconnect to my heart, how to focus on problematic issues and break loose from my self-limiting beliefs. Loretta literally helped me open a door into a brand new way of thinking, feeling and looking at life. I quickly developed confidence and became empowered in so many ways. I am now able to appreciate what I have. I understand that the only limitations in my life are the ones that I create. I was amazed to see how easily my dream life was manifesting!

Within a few weeks my life changed from being a sit-at-home writer, plodding away on my website, to a gregarious, outgoing person. Now I was setting worthwhile goals and accomplishing them. I was happy! I realized that I'd been hiding behind my laptop for years. These days I have a good income, meet lots of people and provide consultation to clients about investments, real estate, etc.

I also advise families who are considering moving to Bali and starting a new life. I listen carefully and answer their questions. I have learned to trust my intuition, which provides me with solutions to their problems. I often form friendships with my clients and this has proven to be a very rewarding experience.

> "With Jacqueline's help and her desire to always understand the needs of her clients, she found the perfect location and villa for us. Happily we have moved and we can say that our quality of life is wonderful. To become not only clients but also friends has made our experience with property hunting to property purchase successful and satisfying. It's a true pleasure to have a competent, reliable and sincere person to assist us."
>
> ~ Dianne Clifton

I have learned how to express myself. I enjoy sharing my ideas and dreams with others. My exuberance and passion for living is contagious and I often find myself in the company of like-minded and like-hearted people. Now that I have become the person I always wanted to be, my goal is to start my own Holistic Retreat Center and teach others what I have learned. My heart is filled with joy. I am grateful for the way my life has developed and how it continues to unfold.

> "Believe in the impossible, and the incredible will become true."
>
> ~ Walt Disney

If you are looking for Rapid Change, it's time to tune into your intuition!

Massimo Pigliucci explains in his book, "Answers for Aristotle: How Science and Philosophy Can Lead Us to a More Meaningful Life:"

"The word intuition comes from the Latin intuir, which means 'knowledge from within...' It works effortlessly (even though it does use a significant amount of brain power) and it's fast. Rational thinking, on the contrary, is analytical, requires effort, and is slow."

We have been taught to suppress or disregard the initial (fast) thought and second-guess by using our rational, analytical mind. My mission is to help busy heart-centered women who want to be the best version of themselves, by showing them how to make Rapid

Changes in their lives. The first step is to properly open the channels of communication between the intuitive and rational mind.

Here are 8 practical tips to help women get un-stuck and move forward with confidence and joy into the life of their dreams:

1. **Stop convincing yourself that you are stuck.** I had a conversation with a friend the other day and she said, "I'm too old, I need money to do this, my mother needs me." Write down your reasons for not moving forward and study them. It is imperative that you identify the obstacles that are holding you back before you can begin working on yourself.

2. **Listen to your inner voice.** Make it a daily exercise to communicate with your intuitive mind. Listen to your intuition, relax and practice rhythmic breathing.

3. **Trust your intuitive mind.** Ask yourself how you are feeling at the beginning of each day, and if the feeling is not good, replace it with a positive thought at that moment. Imagine a comfortable bed, your loving husband, your children, or anything else that brings a smile to your face. Be grateful for the good things in your life.

4. **Allow yourself to be happy.** Pamper yourself. You have a right to be happy, so enjoy a coffee or tea in the morning, and start your day off with a smile. Relax and listen to your intuitive mind before you head out into the hectic world.

5. **Ask questions.** If a situation or experience doesn't feel right, trust that your intuition is warning you. Examine the situation you're in and reconsider the choices you have made or would like to make.

6. **Set your Goals.** Without goals, very little can be accomplished. Write down your short-term and long-term goals, and review them on a regular basis. Monitor your progress and be positive.

7. **Reward yourself.** Give yourself a great big hug every time you achieve a goal. Reward yourself in a way that makes you feel good because you deserve it.

8. **Ask for help.** Never think you have to do it all by yourself. Ask for help when necessary. Look around and be aware who or what feels right.

With practice you will learn to trust your intuition. Intuition is a vital aspect of your true self. By following its gentle guidance, you will realize your dreams and discover a newfound freedom. Your overall health will improve, and most importantly, you'll learn to love yourself.

You deserve the very best in life, and it all starts with you. Life can be a glorious adventure and a joyous experience for those who trust the guidance of their intuition. There is no better time than now to listen to your inner voice and become the best possible version of yourself!

Rapid Results Whole Self Wheel

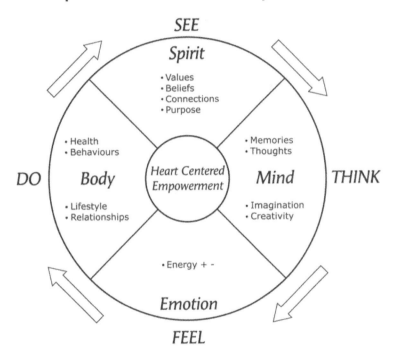

Introduction:
Be the Best Version of You
Physically

The physical potential includes everything that we are: what we do, what we experience, what we choose, and what we communicate. It houses who we are, and when we are fully connected to our body and free of self-deprecating beliefs, we take care of our body. But when we are out of touch with our physical body, which is often the case, we take it for granted, only paying attention to it when it begins to break down – an effect that prevents us from being our best self.

Our physical selves display who we are, what we believe, what we think, and what we feel. And when any one of those behaviors is out of line with the others, it causes an incongruence and disharmony within ourselves. So often people will say, "I'm fine," but display physical signs of anger – slamming a door or speaking in a harsh tone of voice. This incongruence creates tension, both within ourselves and within our relationships; it's like wearing a mask to hide our real self, and it prevents us from being our best self.

To move toward a state of balance, we must identify and transform whatever beliefs are causing us to behave as if our real self does not deserve to exist and look at what experiences created these beliefs.

Michelle Davidson

Michelle Davidson is a board-certified holistic health coach, licensed massage therapist and registered dental hygienist. Her most important and gratifying occupation is being a mom. After navigating her way through divorce, depression and weight gain, she decided to take control of her life. Shortly after, 7 Steps to A.W.E.S.O.M.E™ was born. This program combines Michelle's academic knowledge and life experience to help moms with their biggest and most common challenges. She shares her knowledge and provides support by teaching others how to lose weight, reduce stress and have more energy. Michelle's spiritual, holistic approach to health focuses on diet and exercise, and how they affect personal and professional relationships.

www.theincredimom.com

✉ **michelle@theincredimom.com**

f **facebook.com/theincredimom**

𝕏 **twitter.com/theincredimom**

⊙ **theincredimom**

▶ **youtube.com/theincredimom**

LESSON 23

YOUR FOOD AS FUEL: DISCOVER YOUR NUTRITIONAL STYLE FOR LASTING ENERGY

By Michelle Davidson

The Merriam-Webster dictionary defines energy as:

1. The ability to be active: the physical or mental strength that allows you to do things

2. Natural enthusiasm and effort

3. Usable power

4. Vigorous exertion of power

Synonyms for energy include vitality, vigor, life, zest, spark and exuberance.

In today's fast-paced, complex world, very few people are able to experience joy, vigor and exuberance in their daily lives. Many have become disconnected from the world they live in, are often self-absorbed and lack enthusiasm. I've been there, so I can tell you from personal experience that it's not a good place to be. One day I found myself falling asleep at traffic lights and realized that I had a problem. I'm sure that many of you can relate to this. We all know this is quite dangerous. Feeling tired, run-down and apathetic has become the norm in our society.

I believe that the fact that we can recognize a problem is proof that we can solve it. All answers lie within. It's up to us to make the appropriate adjustments so that we can live a healthy, fulfilling life. Improving the quality and quantity of sleep and exercising on a regular basis are very important, as is proper nutrition.

YOU ARE WHAT YOU EAT

Real food pulses with vitality and biodynamic energy. I'm not speaking about the sterile processed foodstuffs that sit in the middle aisles of your local grocery store. I'm referring to wholesome, natural foods such as vegetables, fruits, nuts, grains and beans that will spoil if left out for too long. This is further indication that it is alive, because microorganisms are able to thrive on it. I'm sure you've seen the video of a fast food hamburger that was left on the counter for 6 months, and still looked the same as the day it was removed from the wrapper. This went viral and caused many people to reconsider the food they were ingesting.

Whole foods are intact and contain vital vitamins, minerals, enzymes and dietary fiber we need, not only to survive but also thrive. When we stray from a diet of living foods, our health degenerates and malnutrition begins to set in. Does lack of energy, depression, irritability and poor concentration sound familiar?

It's important to eat food that is of the highest quality. Food that is grown in healthy soil and a natural environment will be of the highest quality. Organic, wild and biodynamic are some terms used to describe those foods, while conventional and genetically engineered foods are produced by artificial means. Avoid genetically modified organisms (GMOs) and food that has been treated with pesticides, herbicides, and fungicides. Don't consume meats that contain antibiotics and growth hormones such as bovine growth hormone, which is fed to most cattle. The integrity and energy of these foods have been compromised. They affect humans adversely and also pollute our environment.

A healthy diet should consist of a wide variety of foods. I call it "Tasting the rainbow." Food comes in a variety of colors and textures: orange, red, blue, purple, white, yellow, green, etc. Each color indicates the presence of various nutrients, which means you'll be eating a variety of interesting foods. Almonds, kale, citrus fruits, salmon, eggs, curry, berries, ginger and coconut are examples of foods that boost energy levels.

GET INTO THE FLOW WITH H$_2$O

75% of our body is made up of water. Water keeps our cells hydrated and functioning at optimum levels. Many of us are dehydrated which can lead to fatigue, and in the worst-case scenario, can be life threatening. Start off each day with a big glass of water to replace what your body has used up during sleep. Ideally, you should be drinking approximately half of your body weight in ounces. It seems like a lot but you'll get used to it. Keep a cup at your bedside and drink it immediately upon awakening. Make sure that your water is also of the highest quality and free from harmful chemicals. Buying a reverse osmosis filter will do the trick.

The human body prefers to drink water that is at room temperature. Cold water interferes with digestion and prevents the body from absorbing the nutrients in the food that we eat. It also wastes energy because the body needs to regulate the temperature of the liquid. So make sure to hold the ice.

EAT ACCORDING TO THE SEASONS

Mother Nature is very wise. She provides nutritious food when we need it, if we pay attention. Chinese medicine has long recognized that foods and herbs have innate warming and cooling properties. During the summer months, nature provides light, cooling foods such as plums, strawberries, broccoli, summer squash, pears, etc. Autumn signals the arrival of crisp apples and warming foods like carrots, sweet potatoes and onions. In winter it's a good idea to eat warming foods exclusively. Winter squash, potatoes, carrots and other root vegetables are readily available during the cold months. Spring is all about rebirth and renewal. There is an abundance of leafy greens that have cleansing properties. The leafy greens help the body to shed extra pounds that were put on during the winter to provide warmth.

Choosing to eat according to seasons encourages you to eat locally, which means you'll be consuming food that has ripened naturally, and has a high nutrient content. Foods that are shipped long distances are picked before they are ripe to prevent spoilage so that they last longer on the shelf. Did you know the average distance most produce travels from farm to plate is 1,500 miles? And yes, that includes organic. This is very taxing on the environment. If you listen to the call of Mother Nature and eat locally grown food, you'll notice a significant improvement in your overall health.

Meats represent a full range of temperatures. Meats should be consumed in small quantities. If you eat meat, I recommend using it only as a condiment. Again, quality is of the upmost importance. Organic, pasture-raised and grass-fed meats are ideal. Most livestock is raised in stressful and filthy conditions like those in CAFOs (concentrated animal feeding operations). These places are breeding grounds for disease, so the animals are continually given antibiotics to prevent infections. They are also injected with growth hormones to make the young gain weight faster. To make matters worse, they are fed genetically modified ingredients. Remember, you are what you eat.

FILL YOUR MEALS WITH LOVE AND GRATITUDE

Energy is transferred from the cook to the ingredients when preparing food. We're all familiar with the expression, "Made with love." When preparing a meal, use the highest quality ingredients, relax and enjoy the whole experience, because your energy is transferred to those who eat the food you have prepared. Commercial kitchens are very loud and have stressful environments, and this energy is transferred to the food they serve. When dining out, choose small family owned restaurants where good quality food is prepared with care.

WATCH OUT FOR THE LEECHES

Now that we've discussed which foods are the best, when to eat them, and how to prepare them properly, let's discuss foods that deplete your energy and make you ill. I'm glad that I'm explaining this via the written word, because when giving live seminars I always want to duck when I explain the following. Caffeine, soft drinks, alcohol, artificial sweeteners, excess meat, trans fats, coffee, tobacco, milk and processed chemically laden foods are toxic to the human body! There I said it!

I know many people who rely on coffee and sugary snacks to give them a boost, but unfortunately, that's all they get. These substances provide people with artificial energy that is short-lived. These substances deplete the body of vitamins, minerals and are highly addictive. Many people don't realize that sugar and caffeine are drugs that come with several side effects. Not only does consuming these substances make you want more, but also when you stop ingesting them, you'll experience physical withdrawal symptoms.

We have lost our intimate connection with nature. Our food system has changed dramatically, our lifestyles are moving and changing at lightning speeds, and people are suffering. Its time to reclaim our health, replenish our energy and do the things we love. It's time to taste the rainbow and live a joyous life filled with vitality.

Dana Canneto

Dana Canneto is an Energy Healer and Body Awakening™ Transformational Coach. Her intuitive nature and authentic spirit has helped women reconnect with their bodies in such a divine way by supporting them in releasing the falsehoods they carry when it comes to their body and themselves. She shows them how to connect to their body, love their body and nourish themselves on a physical, emotional, mental and spiritual level so they can step into their truth, beauty and purpose.

Today Dana has crafted a beautiful peaceful life sharing her story and gifts with women all over the world.

www.danacanneto.com

facebook.com/danapettitcanneto

danaswellness

pinterest.com/danawellness

linkedin.com/in/danacanneto

LESSON 24

BODY DIVINITY™ – STEPPING THROUGH THE THRESHOLD OF SELF-LOVE AND BODY REVOLUTION

By Dana Canneto

Isn't it time we as women embrace the godliness of our bodies, the beauty of our unique essence and embody the sacred vessel we reside in? Isn't it time to release all the falsehoods we incur as we journey through life feeling as if we are not enough? Isn't it time to rejoice in this sanctified container that drives us through life, that connects us to source and allows us to move about with such grace and ease?

This was not how I looked at my body or my life a little over ten years ago. I was so invested in who I was being judged as rather than simply being who I am.

I remember gazing into the mirror, and looking back at me was this young woman, her face gaunt, and her eyes nearly lifeless. Her brow was heavy in despair, her hair brittle and body so frail. Her joy was completely wrung dry from years of obsession, overindulgence to deprivation and, mustn't we forget, self-loathing.

It was as if I was looking into a stranger's eyes. I was vaguely aware of the tenuous cord tethering my shell to my fragmented mind, body and soul. I can remember asking, "What's happening to me?" and thinking, "I am the victim of a body that is purely against me." Eventually I heard her whisper back, **"No. YOU are against your body."**

Yes, that was I. My spirit being sucked dry of its true essence and my confusion as to where I belonged in the world. What is my purpose? Who am I to become? Who am I to be with? Will I ever be happy with just me? These were the painful years I had to endure to get to where I am now, and for that I feel truly blessed!

I was stripped of pure nourishment on a physical, emotional, mental and spiritual level. My body was my nemesis. I didn't appreciate her nor did I realize she was of any significance to my soul's core. She was this exterior who had to put up a façade of perfection and that all was good in the world, while deep down inside she was aching.

I went from a place of masking my painful emotions by overindulging in food and weight gain towards a place of self-punishment. Stripping myself of the pleasure and enjoyment life is supposed to bring.

I fell for all the pressures of society by living my life according to who I should be rather than who I was… just as I was. I allowed the pressures to define and control my life in every way, not just with my body but the way in which I related to everything in life such as my relationships, my career and my finances.

What if we gave ourselves permission to debunk all the myths of how we should look and just "be?" Remember when you were just a little girl, so curious and innocent? You were simply "you" in your own little world of fantasy and exploration. When I heard my body say to me "No, YOU are against your body," I realized something was wrong. However it wasn't exactly my turning point. I wasn't quite ready to let go yet. I wasn't ready to let go of the victimhood I was living. The "dark night of the soul" moment was when I passed out on my floor a few times and had to call the ambulance on myself. After several days in the hospital and being diagnosed with anorexia, I realized I couldn't live like this anymore.

I began my journey towards healing, and slowly but surely started to regain my strength. I was scared, lonely and had a lot of resistance to being accepted in the world if I truly step into who I am without the perfection I was so striving for. Little did I know, I was even farther from perfect with a 93-pound body on a 5'4" frame. Looking back, life just seemed so hard trying to measure up against everyone else! This was not a short road, as I probed at my body along the way, had a love-hate relationship to food while dealing with fluctuations of weight gain and discomfort, health challenges and setbacks.

Then one day, I woke up and surrendered!! I took all my body woes and handed them over to the Universe. I had no idea what was lying ahead of me but I knew I couldn't take the struggle and pain I was enduring – I just had to trust. Every area of my life was suffering as all my attention was directed to my body and nothing else. I created busy-ness to distract me from having to think or feel. I didn't know how to be in my body and feel safe.

I can proudly say that my body is now my crusader, my soul's delicate encasing whom speaks to me every day with wisdom and charm. She has assisted me in propelling me further towards my purpose in the world, and has shown me the way towards assisting other women with this very fight. I now have a beautiful soulful connection to her. She is my vessel who guides me through life so effortlessly and elegantly as I now live my life through her rather than against her.

I've come to acknowledge how incredibly significant she is to my soul's core. She is not just some exterior hard shell that needs to put up a front of being other than herself.

The body is so sacred. She is the channel to your divine inner knowing. We cannot live our life from a place of truth if we are not connecting to her in this devotional way. She cannot lead us through life when we are filling her up with toxic thoughts, foods and environment. We are simply not leaving enough space for the good to come in, but instead clouding our aura with negativity, self-sabotage and dis-ease.

It's time we, as women, learn to love and accept our bodies just the way they are!

We live in a world today where the woman's body has become such a large part of the conversation, whether in our personal life or in the media. These very discussions have been used as a way to define and control us. How can we blame ourselves for questioning our worth when we are being taught to measure ourselves up against, in some cases the impossible? What IS possible however, is for every woman to get to a place of self-love and adoration for her body and in turn nurture her with beautiful thoughts, food and nourishment in every sense of the word. It was when I chose to clean up my body that I was able to create this beautiful sacred bond with her to where she led me towards a place of freedom within myself.

She is the gorgeous being that envelops your soul and is put on this earth to fully enjoy and experience life while being the truest expression of yourself! I invite you to ask yourself in this moment how you relate to your body? Do you love her? Do you treat her with loving-kindness? Do you nourish her with healthy vibrant whole foods from nature? Do you take care of her or do you take advantage of her?

I have an immense amount of compassion for every woman who continues to struggle with this; for every woman who is trying to "be" something she is not; for every woman hiding behind her true potential for fear of being judged; for every woman sabotaging every relationship she is in because she is so out of love with herself; for every woman who is not living her life's purpose because she doesn't have any energy left to go there; and for every woman who feels powerless and out of control.

What if we as women chose differently despite of all the "shoulds" and just accepted ourselves for who we are. Imagine the example we could be for others, especially for other young women and girls growing up in such a harsh and conflicted world. I now leave you with a few beautiful tips to begin your journey towards loving and accepting the body you are in:

- Acknowledge your body upon waking up by feeling each one of your body parts while sending them love.
- Create a gratitude list before going to bed around your body, giving thanks for each part.
- Play your favorite music and dance in front of the mirror watching her every graceful move.
- Create positive affirmations to offset every negative statement you make towards yourself. Post them somewhere you can see every day.
- Begin to nourish your body with clean wholesome foods while utilizing all of your senses.

- Choose one thing every day that will allow you to truly connect with your body in a new way (i.e., Lathering on coconut oil after the shower)

It's time to love and embrace all of you!

Denise Boisvert

Denise Boisvert is a published author, speaker and entrepreneur. Founder of the unique 10-Step S.L.I.P. System™ that addresses WHY you eat and not just WHAT you eat. The program was inspired by her passion to help women discover and shift their core limited beliefs that keep them trapped in the vicious cycle of weight gain. She personally identifies with the lifelong struggle of weight release and the frustration you feel when the pounds creep back on. Her mission is to conquer obesity one client at a time, by combining visualization techniques that identify the root cause of emotional eating with healthy food education.

Contact Denise:

Austin, TX

www.safelyloseit.com and take my quiz

📞 **(1) 508-294-7881**

🅂 **Deniseb758**

✉ **safelyloseit@gmail.com**

f **facebook.com/safelyloseit**

🐦 **Safelyloseit**

▶ **youtube.com/channel/UCpdMLqIjYT8K1EIbYaQBEcA**

LESSON 25

WEIGHT RELEASE THROUGH BELIEF TRANSFORMATION "VISUALIZATION TECHNIQUES + HEALTHY EATING PLAN = LIFE CHANGING RESULTS"

By Denise Boisvert

The obesity epidemic is one of the country's most serious health problems. Adult obesity rates have doubled since 1980, from 15 to 30 percent, while childhood obesity rates have more than tripled. Research shows that over 95% of people who manage to "lose" weight will gain it back, and most of them will end up weighing more than when they started. Over 200,000 weight loss surgeries were performed in 2013. Gastric bypass surgery is a serious medical procedure that is used to help morbidly obese individuals lose weight. The surgery has a high probability of risks and complications and does not guarantee lifelong weight loss.

The reason patients are susceptible to regaining weight post operation is because the surgery only addresses the biological issues surrounding obesity, and not the mental ones. Most people who reach a morbid level of obesity suffer from binge eating disorders and fundamentally dangerous relationships with food. This is why visualization techniques are crucial to sustaining and maintaining weight release. While helping people with weight release, the numbers of clients who either have had gastric surgery or had been recommended by their doctors to undergo this surgery were not only astonishing but very disturbing. Was this "modern-day fix" just another money maker for the medical industry? I became angry at the thought and decided to do something about it. I started working with clients about WHY they ate, using Visualization Techniques to uncover root causes of their overeating. Together we discovered the underlying emotions or secondary gains associated with their obesity. The results have been astonishing.

I am a firm believer that every "diet" works. I am a **firmer** believer that unless you address WHY you eat, the weight release will only be temporary. It is my mission to conquer obesity one client at a time. To coach my clients through a proven system that transforms their minds and teaches them a healthy eating regimen. I am honored to share with you my approach to weight release. If you noticed, I said weight release and not weight loss. The word "loss" is a negative term, no one likes to lose anything; however when you release something it is most likely a positive freeing feeling. Think about it! When you lose something what happens? You go looking for it. Your subconscious mind is literal and if you lose something you will consciously or unconsciously try to find it.

ARE YOU AWARE YOU HAVE ONE BRAIN – BUT <u>TWO MINDS</u>?

Although we all have one brain, we possess two minds. Our Subconscious mind gives directions based on past experiences, and the Conscious mind follows orders. Through the use of visualization techniques, you can align your conscious desire with your subconscious intention that results in a reality of permanent weight release.

Many times the things we want to "fix" in our lives are things that the subconscious mind controls (smoking, overeating, how we handle relationships, etc.). Visualization techniques can be a great way to manage stress, pain, and weight, in addition to dealing with issues that we just don't know the source of. Sometimes these issues are from things that happened when we were younger and our subconscious linked them to something else that it mistakenly thought was similar. Through visualizations you can make the corrections to bring about the necessary changes.

Many obese people feel that food is controlling them. Lack of control is an illusion. Realize the aspect of yourself that is divine, your Godhood. God is in control of all things, and God is the Self of all, which is your Higher Self. You are the Higher Self. You create all of your reality. There is no aspect of your reality which you do not create. Therefore you control all...

Not being in control makes you feel like a victim. You are not a victim. All power is within and is absolutely under your control. Nothing happens outside of you. Everything is happening within you. You are Consciousness, and Consciousness encompasses All That Is. To create a thing you must want it with a burning desire that allows no denial, backed up by a will that knows no such word as "can't" or "no."

When you focus on what you can do to create what you want, you take back the power. Your intent brings you the knowledge, the awareness and the energy to create what you want. Everything that happens can be traced back to intent...

Visualization techniques are a "Theater in Your Mind" that brings awareness to the WHY you eat so that you can stop self-sabotaging your weight release efforts. They will identify the root cause of why emotions and past experiences have you looking to food for comfort, safety and security. If you truly want to change your life, you must first change your mind. You must free it from the restrictive thinking that holds you back.

Try not to see weight release as your ultimate goal. Instead think about changing your lifestyle, developing a new relationship with food and believing in yourself. Your mind is a powerful fat-busting tool. Use it to see and experience the new healthy, slim version of yourself, and you'll be halfway there.

It's not just about putting in time at the gym and eliminating certain foods; your mental state has a huge influence on whether you hit your weight-release goals. Old thought patterns can seem unbreakable, but moving forward is more possible than you think.

The following are some negative thoughts that may be holding you back from success and what to do about them:

You have negative self-talk: Visualizations work well. Add a ritual of reciting an upbeat mantra and Voila! This is because the intention behind the thought is given meaning and energy by doing something physical to reinforce it. This sends a strong message to the universe and gives you a feeling of empowerment.

You can't imagine the slim you: Once a week spend five minutes looking in the mirror. Take in your entire reflection. Celebrate the things you love about your body, rather than honing in on the things you hate. Once you get into the habit of looking at yourself in this way, you will start to notice all the changes, the small successes that keep you motivated and help you reach your weight loss goal.

You are obsessed with stepping on the scale: Throw away the scale. The number on the scale does not indicate your progress. Actually, the proper eating regimen will most likely result in inches lost before any pounds are shed. Focus your attention on feeling more comfortable in your clothes or having more energy all day long, know that it happened because of your commitment and best efforts.

You are stressed: When our bodies are under stress, we pump out excessive amounts of the hormone cortisol that reduces our ability to burn fat. Even habits that seem healthy can hinder your body from reaching your goal weight. If you're overtraining or overanalyzing every bite of food you take, you can be doing more damage than good. Do your best to find balance in food choices, and keep up with a sustainable workout schedule. These shifts will make a huge difference in the long run, both physically and mentally.

Like it or not, it's survival of the fattest. No visualization is powerful enough to override the survival instinct. Our bodies are programmed, in case of famine, to store fat for future use. That is why it is crucial to learn the science of when to eat along with what to eat.

We are all human and we will "slip up" from time to time. It's OK; actually it just may be a great thing. When you overindulge, it allows you the opportunity to focus on why it happened, and how you could handle it differently in the future. A few "slip ups" here and there will better prepare you for life's inevitable temptations. No need to beat yourself up and let the feeling of failure direct you down the wrong path. Embrace your understanding and celebrate your successes.

The answer lies within. You don't really need another crash diet or the latest appetite suppressant. Weight release is about trusting your innate abilities, as you did when you learned how to walk. You may not remember how scary it was the first time you tried to walk, but you kept getting up until you could do it, without thought or effort. Releasing weight may seem similarly beyond you, but it's just a matter of finding your balance.

Two strategies are better than one. When it comes to releasing weight and keeping it off, a winning combination is visualization techniques and healthy eating regimen.

By reprogramming your mind, you automatically change your thought patterns that have disrupted your weight release efforts in the past. By learning what and when to eat the foods that keep your metabolism burning fat, you experience consistent weight release for a healthier you.

Ariadne Sassafrass

Ariadne Sassafrass is an Empowerment Coach, Energy Transformation Expert, Certified Access Consciousness Facilitator and Conscious Bodyworker. She is highly trained in the gamut of leading edge alternative health and wellness approaches that are grounded in the extraordinary power of Intuition, Psychic and Energetic Awareness. With joy, gentleness and elegance, Ariadne offers up effective tools, techniques and expertise, that can contribute to instantly shifting you from any and all limitation, unease, and dis-ease; while also facilitating you to receive new possibilities and empowering you to create whatever it is you desire to create in and as your life. She travels globally facilitating consciousness. Ariadne has recently created The Elegance of Conscious Living Online Summit Series and is working on her first book. Ariadne offers group classes and private sessions worldwide both in person and online. Ariadne was born with one of the most beautiful parts of Canada, the West Kootenays, of British Columbia, and currently resides on Vancouver Island.

www.accessyourawareness.com

www.eleganceofconsciousliving.com

✉ **ariadne@eleganceofconsciousliving.com**

f **facebook.com/pages/Access-Your-Awareness**

f **facebook.com/pages/Elegance-of-Conscious-Living**

twitter.com/AccessAriadne

LESSON 26

EMBODYING THE SEXUALNESS[1] OF YOU

By Ariadne Sassafrass

I heard a whisper in the darkness, one night alone, in my bed before sleep. *Your beauty doesn't escape me, but envelops me. I hold you without condition, regardless of what you look like or think like. What would it take for you to receive me? I am the space of no judgment, and the pulse that is life, the perceiver and the receiver of you. I am your body and I desire you.*

Do you fully embody the delicious sexualness that you hold? Where is your body in the equation of your life and living? Does thought and thinking propel you forward through your life? Have you, like so many women, shut down or turned off your sexual nature as a result of the objectification of the lovely shapeliness of your body? Do you judge your body continuously because it somehow does not measure up to society's lanky and somewhat anorexic ideals of beauty? Did your mother say that sexual energy was dirty and only sluts enjoyed sex? What other lies did you buy as real that severed you from inhabiting and receiving your body and the sexual energy that it naturally contains?

Throughout history, the female body has been bound, tarred, burned, impregnated, prostituted, utilized and castigated as the reason that begot insanity, dirty sin and evil. The Feminist Movement offered new possibilities for women to exhibit more of who they are outside the stereotypical woman as mother, homemaker and caregiver roles. Though feminism may still have marginalized a woman's full embodiment of sexualness by attempting to categorize and identify

---

[1] Sexualness, though not a word yet found in modern day dictionaries is a conscious construction by the author to suggest a more expansive possibility with one's sexual nature or what has been traditionally defined as sexuality.

her body in relation to a man's or the male's sexual objectification of her.

It wasn't until I was in university that I discovered the ramifications of the projections, judgments, expectations and contortions that were impelled upon the female body. Here I also became aware of how the mind and thought was the impetus for the creation of reality on this planet. In order for thought to exist, a separation occurs from consciousness and the quantum energy that is everything. The thought becomes the other, outside of the thinker; what is perceived as reality is then in relation to its opposite. Polarity became the playing field that enslaved us to separation and limitation. The Mind and everything of it became the measurement of being; the body and everything related to it was seen and viewed as irrational, crazy, unconscious and dirty and sinful. The experience of being in and with a body– and in receiving the energy and the awareness in and of the body – was buried. This energy was sexual – the nurturing, creative, expansive, caring energy that is and creates life. Such conclusions, perpetrated through decades of control and disregard of women's bodies, also contributed to pornography, abuse, objectification, shame, litanies of judgment and a severance of the body from our being.

When I became aware of such travesties, I shut down and hid what was part of the sexual energy that was me. There was no way I was going to let men ogle and objectify me. In this process, I shut down my capacity to receive possibility and create from a space of ecstasy – as orgasmic living begets ecstasy. I often found that my interactions with men created defense, resistance and reaction. I found that I was continuously hiding and keeping myself small. I didn't feel fully alive, and was still someone contributing to the creation of objectification by hiding my body, instead of embodying it. I wondered how it was that there were some women who celebrated their feminine beauty and were impervious to sexual objectification. They exuded a gorgeous, yummy sexual energy that had men eating of their hands, seemingly not bound by sexual politics.

I chose not to feel my body or inhabit my body as the essence that was me. In fact I stood outside my body and was a puppet master, often going through the motions of life. I did not consider the possibility that being in my body, as my body and receiving my body could be a contribution to my life and the catalyst for the creation of an orgasmic living.

It wasn't until I started to learn the tools of Access Consciousness that I began to move beyond the confines of programmed reality (including the resistances and reactions to it) and fully receive the sexual energy, space and consciousness that my body is. Some of these tools included questions and clearing statements that removed the effects of social programming and limitation in my body and entire being, creating more consciousness. I began to have fun with my body; not only did I receive men noticing and admiring my body with ease, my interactions with men were easy and fun. I began to receive more of me. My joy of living increased and I began to tap into the ecstasy of orgasmic living – yes, your day-to-day life can be experienced as one orgasm after another!

Would you like to create a different experience with your body and embody the sexualness that exists within you? Here are some practical and easy-to-use tools that can start to enable you to enjoy the gorgeousness of your female body:

1. Choose a new possibility. Make a demand of yourself that you are going to be, know, perceive and receive all that is you and your body in its entirety. Sexualness is the flow of life that surges through everything: from flowers blooming, to wind caressing and sun warming your skin. OPEN TO THIS. If you become aware of shut-down energy, move into it and turn one molecule of it; it will open into a flow of being that it is.

2. Destroy and uncreate all the lies you bought regarding sex as something dirty and sinful.

3. Start to talk to your body and communicate with it constantly. Your body has its own awareness and consciousness that is beyond any social programming and the unconsciousness of this reality. Choose to be more aware continuously, of what your body is communicating with you; don't just assume and conclude what should be done based on your mind. Choose to commune with your body. Communing takes you out of

thought and thinking and into receiving, into embodiment. From this place of total awareness and full presence in your body you actually move out of the separation of reality into Oneness and total consciousness. You will then be able to receive the contribution of everything to you.

4. Destroy and uncreate all the judgments you have about your body; all of those that you have taken on from others, return back with a little bit of consciousness attached. You showing some flesh, and the beauty of your shape, whether thin, voluptuous, muscular or aged, inspires new possibilities for all.

5. Start to receive the energy of everything just as energy without any judgments or conclusions about what kind of energy it is. This includes men and women adoring your body. Your body actually likes to be lusted after.

6. Start to play with your female body outside of the polarization of your gender. Move beyond the form, structure and significance of your gender differences, and the decisions, judgments, and conclusions that have been impelled upon you, that you may have chosen to resist and react to.

7. Make space in your life to regularly celebrate and escalate the sexual energy of your body, whether it be with yourself, your partner, your lover or lovers. This celebration does not necessarily need to include copulation and orgasm. Our bodies are sensuous and they like being touched, caressed and held. This can be orgasmic.

8. Feel your feet on the ground. Receive the energy of the Earth as a contribution to you and bring that energy up through your body, remembering the flow of orgasm enveloping you. Now continue to receive this energy out the top of your head. Push all of your barriers down (where energetically you have put up walls around you) and now allow yourself to receive the energy of everything contributing to you. Pull this energy to you and through you. In this space, you can begin to receive the energy of whatever you desire.

Your female body has capacities you have not been aware of. If you continue to shut down your body, you shut down your capacity to receive possibility. There is a potency that is the sexualness of you. What if you could create a new reality with this? Be a conductor of the symphonies of the universe, with the flow, pull and draw and all variances in between. What can you create with the flow of your sexualness out into the world – gracing others with the beautiful vibration that is you? Are you willing to be that alive? I dare you!

Tracy Reifferscheid

Tracy is an Intuitive Visionary, transforming and sparking the energy within those around her. She assists you in finding what is missing in your life....YOU!!! Tracy uses many techniques that she has been trained in and developed. She does this with energy and the assistance of many Divine Beings including your own Team and Soul.

She has taken what she has learned and embraced, and offers this to others in one-on-one sessions, distance healing sessions across the world and through workshops in any location. Tracy is a Facilitator of Joy, Empowerment and AWEsomeness infusing these energies in the world around her.

Tracy can be reached in numerous ways:

**Located in Humboldt, SK Box 2943 S0K 2A0
or Saskatoon, SK 3-2228 Ave C North, S7L 6C4**

www.awakeningstherapies.com

📞 **306-231-4350**

Ⓢ **Tracy Reifferscheid**

✉ **tracy@awakeningstherapies.com**

f **Tracy Reifferscheid or Awakenings Therapies**

in **Tracy Reifferscheid**

LESSON 27

ENERGETIC HEALING –
YOU ARE THE CONNECTION

By Tracy Reifferscheid

We are each energetic beings. Each of us has our own unique vibration, and this vibration is interacting with each unique vibration of other people, animals, plants and all things at all times. Our thoughts, feelings, beliefs, food, genetics, other people and electronics all affect this vibration, but we choose how this will affect us. We choose this consciously or subconsciously, through the beliefs and programs that we have running and, most dangerously, while we are on autopilot. When we make our choices while on autopilot, we are doing so based on previous programs and beliefs without using our awareness. When we start making choices based on our awareness, we have engaged ourselves.

My journey began when I had many illnesses and emotional obstacles come up in my life. I had my tonsils removed by age 4, gallbladder removed by age 17. I suffered from teenage and adult acne for most of my life. Endometriosis created so much scar tissue that I would be prevented from having any more children by the age of 21, along with numerous surgeries to cure me of this disease. My emotions, mental state and body were suffering and in pain. Many days were spent focused on all that was wrong with my body and medicating the pain and symptoms. These were just some of the things I suffered from physically.

I suffered from anxiety that at times created so much fear and more illness. I did a really great job of hiding my anxiety from most people for many years, until I had to take a leave of absence due to stress from my job. Although I was able to blame others for this. Before I moved on, that was the EXCUSE I used, that I latched on to, even though I wasn't consciously aware of it being an excuse.

No one is responsible for how I feel. Did I have experiences in my life? Yes! What some would classify as tragic-yep. I experienced abuse of different types, grew up in an alcoholic home, have a learning disability called dyslexia, was a teenaged unwed mother as well as other experiences. I only share those to say that yes they existed. What I have learned is that I get to choose what I hold on to and what I don't. Every time I blamed someone or something else, I gave a bit of myself away as well as my own personal power. My emotional, mental and spiritual states were so removed from the Infinite Being that I am, that it created physical and emotional blocks. I was so far removed from myself that I didn't even know I had a self. I functioned from everything that I was told consciously or subconsciously throughout life from societal systems, friends, family, genetics and more. To the point that I really had no connection to myself, to Tracy.

As I child, I remember asking questions about everything; I remember being shut down for asking questions. I then created a pattern of don't ask because that is an annoyance, that it made people angry, that made me stand out. I also worked hard at being invisible. As time went on, the less I questioned the less I expanded or grew. The more I went on autopilot, the less I existed, and I questioned even less. This created a circle that then was manifesting as disease, unhappiness and a disconnection to life.

Then a wonderful thing happened without me even realizing at the time. I started asking questions again. I started to ask what I could do to be healthier; what I could do to be happier. I could stop blaming my mom for the genetics I inherited. I could stop blaming my parents for stuff in my childhood; I could stop hating and blaming the man that assaulted me. I was holding on to so much anger that I had stuffed down into my body that I didn't even know I had. I had learned to stuff things down; what I had to say didn't count, I didn't know how to communicate. I stopped really feeling, and made choices and decisions based on what I thought society and others expected of me. I felt that until I got angry, no one understood me.

My husband pushed me out of this box, by just accepting, loving and supporting me. He asked me questions; he noticed how I was so detached from my upbringing. He said to me one day, "When you talk about your childhood it sounds like you are talking about someone else. You have no emotional reaction." This got me asking questions about myself, which took me even deeper to finding so much more than I knew existed.

This led me to energy work. I have always felt energies around me but I had shut this down. I would run my hands over my husband's body saying I know I should feel where you hurt or where something isn't right. I always knew at some level that I have the capability to heal myself. So my journey began into Energy work and re-opening all my Intuitive abilities that I had shut down. I learned to run energy in the form of Reiki. There are other many wonderful energy techniques, but Reiki is what resonated with me. This is my foundation, and Reiki opened me up to a whole different world of possibilities. When I chose to allow myself to heal and to be open to healing myself with Reiki, I became more of who I truly am, an Infinite Being. Even though at the time I had no idea that is who or what I was. The energy shifted me, and I started to choose to allow myself to heal. My physical body started to heal and release the disease, illness and pain that it was holding. My emotional and mental body was healing. I reconnected to my own awareness, intuition and physic abilities.

I started to recreate Tracy. I had no idea who I was but I knew who I wanted to be. So I asked, "What do I need to change to be this person?" Little did I know that every question I asked brought new people, situations and energies into my world. Although in the beginning, I also tried to answer these questions. What I know today is that by being in the question, allowing it to show up in my life in the best way possible, I allow my Awareness to direct me.

You may be asking the question, "How do I follow my Awareness?" This is a process that anyone can learn, and I now teach others how to embrace their own gifts and talents, whether they are aware of them or not. I teach others how to run energy and how to sense it through their own unique talents and sensory abilities. Whether you are aware or not, EVERYBODY has the ability to be aware to work within energy and most of all to HEAL themselves.

I decided one day that holding others responsible and being angry at them was only affecting my life. What did I need to change? I started my journey into forgiveness; I started by forgiving all those in my life that I held accountable for all the bad things. If I wanted to love myself, I realized I needed to embrace all those parts of my past as they contributed to the person I was. Then I had an Awakening. My questions led me to the awareness that I only need to forgive myself – not anyone else. By saying I forgave someone else was me still saying that person was responsible for how I feel. I was giving my power away. I forgave myself for the fear and aloneness I felt as a child for hiding that beautiful little girl's energy. I forgave myself for not getting myself out of a situation that led to an attack. I thanked myself for all the strength that I had shown. I forgave me for not loving and embracing me.

I have since learned how to let go of my limiting beliefs and patterns. I now share this in sessions and workshops with others. I see the beauty within each person and their vibrant energy that is asking to be released. I do this in Soul coaching sessions, Reiki and Access Consciousness. I listen to what your soul is saying and communicating with you. If you haven't yet learned to hear the whispers or sometimes shouts of your soul, know that you have the ability to. You have the ability to heal from anything, there are infinite possibilities within. You ARE an infinite being with infinite capabilities!!!

Michele Kralkay, DNM RHN

Michele Kralkay, DNM RHN, is a complementary medical practitioner, health consultant, lecturer, and best selling author. She runs a successful practice in Saskatoon and welcomes the opportunity to train interested groups. In addition to using natural whole foods, Michele uses a well-rounded approach when guiding her patients to optimal health, either in person or through distant healing. Michele is a Doctor of Natural Medicine and a Registered Holistic Nutritionist. She is also educated and certified in Theta Healing, Quantum Touch, Thought Field Therapy, Systemic Enzyme Therapy, Dowsing, Energy Healing, Sports Nutrition, Electro Dermal Screening, Orthomolecular Medicine and Homotoxicology.

Contact her at:

www.buildhealthnaturally.com

(1) 306-477-4480.

buildhealthnaturally@gmail.com

facebook.com/michele..kralkay

twitter.com/MicheleKralkay

LESSON 28

HEALING FROM THE CAUSE
By Michele Kralkay, DNM RHN

We go through life seeking answers to questions such as… Why am I as I am? Why do I feel the way I feel? What makes me sick? Why do I repeat the same patterns of behavior? Why am I not happy? What is wrong with me? What is the nature of my negative thoughts? What is the cause of my illness? We often seek solutions in the form of therapies and medications, which may have limited results or even make matters worse.

Most people seek health care when faced with pain or some other form of dis-ease. Many symptoms, particularly acute and physical ones, can often be effectively treated on the symptom or syndrome level with material interventions. Yet often, particularly in chronic, recurrent or nonphysical conditions, the need arises for heightened understanding of the cause and of how to more strongly call upon intrinsic sources of health and harmony. In this way, illness or discomfort can guide us to seek and find a more complete state of health. When we find the superior equilibrium that resolves the symptoms, the illness has been healed and we are something more than we were before, in a state of greater health and well-being.

"Let food be thy medicine and medicine be thy food."

~ Hippocrates

I have a strong belief that the quality of what we put into our bodies – food, air, movement, water, sleep, thoughts, and experiences – has a major impact on our health and well-being. We need to look at how we are nourishing ourselves in the broadest sense, not just from food. As multidimensional beings, we can draw nourishment from all activities, encounters and interactions with anything that has a vital energy. Food, people, nature, inanimate objects and yes, even rocks.

Primary sources of nourishment are loving and supportive relationships, meaningful work, physical exercise, and spiritual/ mindful practices. Food provides the essential nutrients necessary to support life and health, but is a secondary source of nourishment in this expanded sense. The way in which we nourish ourselves is also a deep reflection of how we perceive ourselves and how much we value life in this form. It's a depiction of our limitations, but also our potential.

When I started my formal education and natural medicine practice almost 20 years ago, natural medicine, in particular holistic nutrition and energy medicine, were not well known. In fact, I would say they were even feared, doubted and dismissed. There were no foundations in place. Thus, I became a pioneer. My quest to marry holistic nutrition, energy therapies, ancient healing modalities, innate wisdom and conventional medicine into integrative practice was just a dream. People were talking about the body-mind connection, but there was a faddish approach. There were many questions, roadblocks and so much convincing to be done. However, I just knew, deep down in my soul, I was on the right path.

> "When health is absent
> Wisdom cannot reveal itself
> Art cannot manifest
> Strength cannot be exerted
> Wealth is useless and
> Reason is powerless."
>
> ~ Herophiles 300 BC

My health "suddenly" failed in 1997. Misinterpreting the signals my body was giving me, I turned to conventional medicine for help. For the next six months I literally fought for my life. I used alternative and complementary therapies to heal myself from the iatrogenic disease and in turn was also able to reverse several of the chronic conditions I had developed to that point of my life. I thought my struggle for optimal health was over. Not so!

"It is a lot easier to maintain health than it is to rebuild health."

I had learned a valuable lesson and was set on my path to help others. Being a naturally inquisitive person with a gift of retaining learned and acquired knowledge, I delved into the world of "natural medicine and healing." I developed a long list of educators, teachers and associates. Each one of them awakened gifts I had forgotten I had. I was on a mission to help bring as many people to optimal health as possible, either as a healer, a connector or as a guide.

Some of the most valuable lessons reveal themselves over and over again. We each have the power within us to heal to our most optimal level of health and well-being. My path – not an easy one – showed me how I could teach others to discover this power and how to use it.

THE LAW OF CURE

From above, downwards.
From within, outwards.
From a more important organ to a less important one.
In the reverse order of their coming.

~ Dr. Constantine Hering

To heal rapidly, an intense investigation into the path that led to illness must not be overlooked. Can you pinpoint an event or time in your life that you can target when your health began to change? An experienced natural health practitioner can guide you through this process. Once the path to a cause is found, layers will be peeled back, one by one. Sometimes a person can shed several layers in a day, week or month. And that same person may take months or years just to get through a more complex layer. Often there is more than one semi-cause leading to the main cause.

"Health is not the absence of disease, but the ability to overcome it."

~ Anonymous

A woman sought me out to help her with a myriad of complicated and ongoing symptoms she'd had for about the last six months.

These included headaches, fatigue/exhaustion, digestive upsets, sleeplessness, moodiness, apathy, joint pain, and a feeling of general deterioration in all body systems. She had been to many conventional medicine practitioners who had all deemed her healthy through their testing; however, she remained on sick leave from work. Even though no cause had been identified, she had been prescribed a plethora of medications to treat the symptoms. These brought no relief and deepened her concern about what was going on.

She arrived at her initial appointment with a support person. She knew she needed to change what she was doing and was ready to do what it took. The initial appointment involved a full body assessment and analysis, and the commencement of a healing protocol that included diet and lifestyle recommendations; supplements, herbals, and homeopathy; an introduction to energy modalities; and "homework" to be completed by the next appointment, usually in a month.

This woman went home with her path to make significant advances with her health. About five days later, I received a phone call from her support person reporting that her friend had improved dramatically, so much so that she was already back to work. She could not believe how quickly the few changes she had made so far reversed her most debilitating symptoms. I encouraged the support person to make sure this woman sticks to her path.

This woman is typical of the patients I see. The body gave her signals something was wrong. She was not responding with proper nourishment and care, so the symptoms increased in severity. Her difficulty with her digestive system also indicated her difficulty digesting her life. She needed validation and direction. She needed a path that would empower her to trust in her own innate wisdom and successfully peel back the layers to get to the cause.

I gave her a short course on interpreting body signals. I taught her an easy way to connect with her innate wisdom. I guided her through her diet cleanup. I gave her movement exercises that would release some of the pent up emotions along with the pain she experienced. And I gave her tools to deal with the stress she was encountering on a daily basis.

The most powerful single tool I use in my practice supports the body when dealing with stress, provides a release for pent up emotions, and empowers the person to trust in their own choices. I call this mindful breathing.

1. Start by focusing on an area of pain or health concern. Determine the level of dis-ease on a scale of 1 (little) to 10 (unbearable).

2. Using a method of muscle testing you are comfortable with, determine if now is an appropriate time to work with your body to release this health concern. If yes, then…

3. Remember to ground yourself; open your heart energy by focusing on it and inhale using a deep belly breath.

4. Envision your body healing or healed as your cells take in the breath.

5. Exhale – releasing what no longer serves you.

6. Repeat steps 3 to 5 for approximately 5 minutes. Recheck with step 1 ensuring an improvement. Repeat process if necessary.

7. Practice this daily until you can do this while walking. Include it with your 20 minute stress relief walks.

The personal lessons I learned along with the clinical experience of working with thousands of patients through almost two decades have made me the healing practitioner I am today. Never being satisfied, my personal quest for optimal health is ongoing.

Brenda Young

Brenda's book **The Divine Shift** (2011) is a Conversation with Creator account of our world's transformational journey from duality to unity consciousness. Her soon-to-be released book **Return to Gaia ~ Talk with the Goddess** is an integral healing journey, channeled through the Divine Feminine.

An **Intuitive Energy Healer**, Brenda uses many integrative healing modalities. She walks the Shamanic path and is an Obsidian Pipe Carrier.

Brenda also facilitates women's healing circles and is a **Spirit Guide**. She's now launching her **Luminous Leader** mastery program. She leads a holistic lifestyle on the beautiful Sunshine Coast of BC, Canada.

www.spiritguide.ca

- 604.720.6407
- spiritguide333
- brendayoung333@gmail.com
- Brenda@spiritguide.ca (as of June 11, 2014)
- facebook.com/pages/The-Divine-Shift-Brenda-Young/621450734563216
- linkedin.com/profile/view?id=31897328&trk=nav_responsive_tab_profile_pic

LESSON 29

RETURN OF THE GODDESS

By Brenda Young

Today's high-powered hectic lifestyle is stress city. Work, kids, partners, pets and aging parents leave little time for the self. If this is the age of the empowered woman, why are we suffering from brain drain, body burnout and soul starvation?

If time is the new currency, then balance is today's prize. The female overachiever icon on a tightrope with a title, technology, and tidy home is as worn out as she is. The self-realized woman is one who prioritizes her self – is grounded, centered, and plugged in.

But how do we integrate and anchor health, overcoming daily demands? A male personal trainer provided the answer. "Women know what to do to stay healthy. What stops them is lack of self-love." Truth! I've vested enormous energy into family, career and community but taken little time to nurture myself; a role model we're all transcending to re-write "herstory." After watching my female ancestors burn through women's lib movements, fight for the right to vote, and myself, compete in a male-driven work world, we've come full circle.

Originally, we were revered medicine women and shamans of an ancient order, in harmony with our bodies, earth and cosmos. We had rituals. We alchemized elements. We chanted and embodied this energy, dancing under the moon. Then, we were shut down to facilitate a patriarchy. And we've been suffering since. Finally, we're reclaiming our power.

We're all healers, connected mythically to the goddess. Now we're returning to this embodiment of self-love, self-acceptance and self-nurture as essential truths. We're reviewing our stories, refocusing our values, and reclaiming what was lost or suppressed, to recreate our lives from our highest purpose.

As an intuitive healer, I've recalled how to get in touch with my emotions, to access my inner radiance, and to build healthy relationships with my body, beloved, community and the earth. It's resulted in liberation and profound self-love. When I feel this, I want to sing, dance, drum, create and celebrate, linking the sky, heart and feet to the earth as we women did in circles so long ago.

This year in Costa Rica, I did just that, part of a Moon Dance with 200 women, ceremonially circling for four nights straight, dressed in white. A beautiful corona from herbs, eucalyptus and fresh mums I made adorned my crown. White ribbons trailed from my wrists. My eyes bright, my heart song strong, my hips swaying, I danced my prayers as the drum beat steadily. I found my joy and ecstasy mirrored in hundreds of women who twirled with me, for the sheer bliss of reunion of earth, moon, and each other, under the heavenly starlight. I enthusiastically pulled my sandals off, to come into full contact with Mother Earth, to kiss her with my toes!

Ground is not dirt, but our mother, sacred and beautiful, I beamed, as I found my way back to my tent after morning sweat lodge, flopping myself down; my belly pressing next to hers.

The goddess is awakened in us. We know that the Holy Grail of self-acceptance we sought – but never found – doesn't exist. It's not in our business achievements, sexual desirability or ability to conform. It is in us. Is it is any wonder we were sick and tired?

The men have suffered too, discouraged from displaying feminine qualities. Until we can balance our feminine and masculine aspects – fire and fluidity – as the sun and the moon cooperate, we cannot be well. It's now time for the body's intuition to speak, the healer within. We can't quash this wellspring and library of truth within us, repressing energy in our lower chakras dealing with security, sexuality and power, and get well.

Yet I learned long ago not to express resentment or anger – or any "negative" emotion – when that may have been the catalyst to mobilize my health. With that uncirculated energy trapped and reverberating, unable to connect to my diaphragm, how could I give my wisdom a voice? This type of denial can sink a woman's self-esteem, worthiness and self-confidence when she feels exploited but can't express her feelings of entrapment. Shut down, the result is often some form of debilitating disease, deemed as incurable, mystifying doctors.

The body is a beautiful barometer. Symptoms signal in the same way our shadow selves show us where we've strayed from self-love. If we can stop fearing, judging and hating these cues, we can begin to appreciate our experiences and our bodies, designed to cooperate with our environment. In the same way, we can understand Mother Nature's signs showing us we're out of balance, in jeopardy. By honoring our intuition and moon nature, we find our most vital light shimmering on the deep waters of our own compassion.

When we suffocate this empathetic relationship, we have the world we have today, full of malaise. We're out of balance. Aboriginal people have said, "What we do to our Mother, we do to ourselves." First Peoples stories are emerging for reconciliation, with tales of exploitation and violation. It's now time for healing – both mother and inner child – to restore us all. We can't silence signs that the earth has gone past the tipping point, denying our relationship to her, treating symptoms but denying root causes.

We've buried stories of ancient priestess cultures that honored nature's cycles, organic health and cosmic relationships to support a system that does not support us. We've applauded scientific and clinical research, yet we're still out of touch with our roots. We've done so at the expense of the phenomenal wisdom of our heart, reducing it to an organ pumping blood. Yet our heart is a vital doorway to our evolving consciousness, with potential answers to every modern-day problem. Instead, we've tried to cure heart disease the way we regulate every other system in our world, in a masculine way.

Our hearts have been captive, plagued with deep wounds and grievances, some storing memories of heinous crimes from this lifetime or another. Yet the heart is our greatest teacher, steadily pumping, asleep or awake. Like a dance, our heart beats rhythmically;

receptive and directive flow synergistically, a lesson in openness and cooperation. A heart first beats in an unborn fetus before a brain is formed. What then, signals a heart to beat, if not a connection to greater intelligence?

How many cadavers must we dissect and particles must we collide to find a truth stored in our own smart heart? The secret revealed is balance. This poise and grace is reflected in all nature. It's an equilibrium designed to sustain life. Harmony can only be maintained through honoring this truth. Nature gave us two eyes with one vision. Now we can use insight to bring us home to homeostasis. Wisdom can temper action.

That is why the Dali Lama said, "It will be the western woman to save the world." We cannot heal our bodies or planet without feminine wisdom. We come from the mother and return to her. Now we must listen to her. We're now embracing emotional health and holistic treatment. Alternative health continues to lead us back to our body's innate intelligence and ability to self-heal.

The caduceus, a medical symbol, says much about this transformation. The two snakes, representing masculine and feminine, show balance. They can be seen as shedding outdated prescriptive formulas and teachings to embody holistic knowledge. Atop is the phoenix, a symbol of our own evolution, as we arise from the ashes of ignorance into optimal health.

We women are the leaders, visionaries and healers pioneering the future of wellness to help balance the forces of nature. How long must we sacrifice, diminish and dishonor ourselves? We are powerful. Let's embody our worth and allow our emotions to feed us trust instead of crucify us with self-doubt. Like Mother Earth, we've been commoditized to uphold society's dark illusions. And from this ground, we've grown. Our light has risen, like a star from a seed. We know our deep truth, and can now bask in this radiance. We are free now to reclaim our health, creativity and soul. We're all sisters, not competitors for a job title. We've been lied to. We're a circular bond of strength and unity, connected to one womb, one web.

Moving away from a world of ladder climbing, our unified message and greatest power is compassion. It is our safe haven, strengthened through reunion, the balanced male and female within. As we honor the earth's cycles and womankind, we're like a great hurricane, a change agent in the world, demanding transparency, honor and healing.

For the first time in eons, we can feel safe. The goddess has returned to bring balance, empowering us through unity and love. We can now act, sharing our truth with a world that needs us for her survival, and the continuation of life. When we honor this, we declare our worth, wisdom, and leadership. We are free to liberate our selves and all who touch our light.

Conclusion:

Bringing All the Levels Together

Kathy Friedberg Bloom

Kathy Friedberg Bloom has worked in Corporate America for almost 30 years in a variety of capacities including technical work, organizational effectiveness, program management, and local and global Human Resources. Her passion has been to find creative ways to bring holistic healing into the workplace – person by person. Balance is her number one priority which she works to achieve through personal awareness, utilizing her simple 4-step process, setting intentions, the power of positive thinking, essential oils and gemstones, healing touch, and meditation.

Contact Kathy:

 skarbloom@aol.com

BRINGING IT ALL TOGETHER: ACHIEVING BALANCE

By Kathy Friedberg Bloom

Balance. We all strive for it, but most of us struggle to achieve it. I know from my own experience that even with the best intentions, given today's fast paced world and the myriad of obligations we each face, balance often eludes us. With some close examination of what is important in our lives and a few alterations in how we think and prioritize, we can begin a new journey. Right now. Right this very moment.

I have learned the importance of maintaining balance through my own life experiences. I am the mother of two children; both my parents and extended family live close by. I work full time in a large global company with high expectations. I run my household and am responsible for its daily upkeep. There are family medical issues which require my time and energy, and I have my own health goals I am working towards. I have many friends and live in a wonderful community in which I try to find time to volunteer and connect. I want to be fully devoted to ALL of it. Just listing all of the things I juggle makes me feel tired and out of balance. Regardless of what they are, we all have challenges which can result in severe consequences if something gets ignored. Balance is crucial to keeping our lives in order.

When I am not in balance, I realize that I do not feel inner peace, connectedness and joy. I do not perform at my best in either my personal life or my work life. I end up neglecting certain aspects of my life and I feel vulnerable, as if my life were spinning out of control. When we are in balance, we are able to deal with any situation – good or bad – using all of our senses, heart and soul in the most efficient and effective way possible… and with grace. So why do we continue to allow ourselves to be sidetracked from keeping balance in our lives? I believe that we gravitate towards the things that come most easily and naturally to us, which refers to those activities that give us the least amount of resistance. We need to move out of our comfort zones and create new pathways for ourselves so that we can maintain the ever important balance we crave.

To understand the importance of balance, let's take a look at what it means to be out of balance using a simple analogy. As we are all familiar with four-wheeled vehicles, begin by focusing on the tires. Imagine that one tire is overinflated and about to burst, one tire is completely flat, one is properly inflated and the last has half its needed air. How would the car move with these four tires? Not very well! Now let each of the tires represent one of the quadrants in your life – the physical, spiritual, mental and emotional quadrants. How do you operate when your four "tires" are out of balance? Imagine the extra effort you must exert to complete even the simplest of tasks. Now that you have this vision in your mind, let's begin to address how to achieve balance. I use a four step process.

Four Steps to Achieve Balance

- Assess
- Identify
- Prioritize
- Start/Stop/Continue

First, complete an honest assessment of where you currently are in each quadrant. Continuing with the car analogy, you could use the following ratings with the goal of being "just right." We are not striving for perfection, just balance.

- Flat
- Slightly under-inflated
- Just right
- Slightly over-inflated
- About to burst

If you are slightly over-inflated in one quadrant and slightly under-inflated in another, that is okay – your car will still run with a small variance in the pressure of the tires. The operative phrase here is "small variance."

Next, identify the top three activities you perform on a daily or weekly basis to support each quadrant. Make them tangible and realistic given your schedule. An example from my life looks like this.

- Physical – Yoga, Walking my dog, Exercising
- Spiritual – Meditation, Attending services, Reading
- Mental – Sudoku, Work challenges, Learning new skills
- Emotional – Date nights with my husband, Journaling, Sunday night dinners with my family

Next, <u>prioritize</u> each of the activities in order of their importance to you – "A" being the highest priority and "C" the lowest. You can use this prioritization to help determine activities that you need to add to your schedule and those you need to either remove or reduce the frequency. For instance, I am often very overinflated in the mental quadrant and need to reduce the amount of time I spend on the lowest priority activities, in order to create time for one of the higher priority activities in the physical quadrant which is underinflated for me.

Last, complete the <u>START/STOP/CONTINUE</u> step. Ask yourself, "Which activities do I need to start doing, which activities do I need to stop doing and which activities do I need to continue doing?"

By evaluating your current focus and writing down your priorities, you have already begun your journey towards balance.

Performance Ratings at work – A new way of thinking in the 4-quadrant model of balance:

The mental quadrant is generally one where people naturally tend to focus. I have worked in the corporate world for almost 30 years and often have the opportunity to discuss people's disappointment with their performance ratings. Many factors contribute to this disappointment: relative rankings, complexity of assignments, peer group evaluations, scope/reach of projects, to name just a few. The most critical component to our disappointment is the importance that each of us place on how we are rated – either by ourselves or someone else. However, performance ratings are most likely focused solely on one quadrant – the mental quadrant. Using the 4-quadrant model helps put the evaluation into perspective. If you are someone who has ever felt disappointment with your performance – either though your own personal evaluation of your efforts or through someone else's evaluation – I challenge you to refocus your "performance goal" towards achieving the "highest performance rating" possible in the BALANCE OF YOUR LIFE, across the mental, physical, spiritual and emotional quadrants. Refocusing in this way gives you a new sense of self-worth and a feeling of doing something you can control for yourself. It is actually quite simple. If you are in balance, you are experiencing life to the fullest and in the most joyful way. When you are living fully and joyfully, you attract more of the same in your life which continues to enhance all of your interactions and contributions. And the best part is... you are in control! You are the only one who can make the decisions appropriate for your balance, because you are the only one who can define what balance means to you. Once you define your balance and work towards achieving it, all of the aspects of your life become more manageable.

Achieving balance could be the most important thing for us all, yet we all still struggle with achieving it. Need some ideas for how to do this? Identify the quadrant(s) for which you need more support and re-read those chapters in this book. See which ideas resonate best with you. When the four wheels of your vehicle are in balance, imagine the possibilities! Which path will you choose to take now? Which looks interesting for future exploration? To which road signs will you pay attention and which will you consciously choose to ignore? Create new pathways for yourself and identify fun ideas and side trips to pursue. Experience joy in the process. Hold the intention to create and achieve balance, and let the universe do its work to help guide you in the direction that is right for you.

My wish for you is to achieve balance in your four quadrants, so that you may experience physical vitality, emotional stability, mental clarity and alignment with Spirit.

TESTIMONIAL

I elected to be part of this wonderful journey with 30 other women to find new pathways and have a positive impact on the lives of people by helping them understand both the importance of achieving balance in their lives and some simple techniques for doing so.

Conclusion

I hope you enjoyed getting to know each unique author through her story! I don't know about you, but for me, being exposed to other people's views and techniques is life altering. And I hope that's what this book has been for you.

The benefits and empowerment of collaboration are endless; you tapped into the knowledge of 30 women to broaden your horizons, raise your conscious level, and learn from other's experiences. Know that through all of this, rapid change is possible and that understanding the four aspects of yourself through the Whole Self model shows you how and why it is possible.

Some final tips to awaken the best version of you: Make the time to allow for new discoveries and opportunities; call upon the Universal Source, Creator, God, for guidance in all areas to make life more efficient; allow yourself to explore your inner thoughts so you can achieve a greater sense of awareness and meaningfulness; play full-out; and shed your fears by seeing your truth.

This is a time of great self-discovery and transformation for you. As you work to manifest your best possible self, you will see things from a deeper perspective than ever before, so make it your intent to make your life priority. After all, you're worth it. Open and connect to your heart-centered consciousness daily, and you will naturally transform all the old, outdated beliefs you have about yourself into beliefs aligned with the best version of you. Remember, *that* you is already within you and by reading and re-reading the chapters in this book, it will help awaken that new you.

In Wholehearted love, and light,

Loretta Mohl

An 11 Step Recipe
for a Fulfilling Life

Most likely, if you have picked up this book it means that you are either tired of being stressed out, feeling lost or overwhelmed or you have the impression of spinning your wheels. So you may be thinking that there is no hope and desperation may be engulfing you as if it was the only way out.

To experience a fulfilling life you need to have goals. Why? Because they are the steps on the escalator of life which take you from not knowing what's wrong with you to feeling high on life.

But you may not even consider goals right now…. because all you can feel is frustration. You are stuck in a rut!

I think I have the perfect solution for you. My 11 step program is based on my 25 years of experience working with women who felt just like you do today. The Results? They understood why they felt stuck, they discovered what they were doing (or not doing) to feel so lost and then, most important of all, they learnt what to do to regain control of their life to finally be able to live a happy and fulfilling life.

If your happiness is really important to you, please copy the link below into your URL and come talk to me. I know I can make a difference in your life starting from today.

Website: http://www.lorettamohl.com

The End